a GOD-CENTERED worldview

Matt Chandler, Afshin Ziafat,
Mary Jo Sharp, J. D. Greear, and more

THE
GOSPEL
PROJECT
FOR ADULTS

LifeWay | Adults

Ed Stetzer General Editor Trevin Wax Managing Editor

No part of this work may be reproduced or transmitted in any form or by any means, electronic or mechanical, including photocopying and recording, or by any information storage or retrieval system, except as may be expressly permitted in writing by the publisher. Requests for permission should be addressed in writing to LifeWay Press®, One LifeWay Plaza, Nashville, TN 37234-0102.

ISBN: 978-1-4300-2942-7
Item: 005606814

Dewey Decimal Classification Number: 220.07
Subject Heading: BIBLE—STUDY \ THEOLOGY—STUDY \ GOSPEL—STUDY

We believe that the Bible has God for its author; salvation for its end; and truth, without any mixture of error, for its matter and that all Scripture is totally true and trustworthy. To review LifeWay's doctrinal guideline, please visit *www.lifeway.com/doctrinalguideline*.

Unless otherwise noted, all Scripture quotations are taken from the Holman Christian Standard Bible®, copyright 1999, 2000, 2002, 2003, 2009 by Holman Bible Publishers. Used by permission.

To order additional copies of this resource, write to LifeWay Church Resources; One LifeWay Plaza; Nashville, TN 37234-0113; phone toll free (800) 458-2772; fax (615) 251-5933; email *orderentry@lifeway.com*; order online at *www.lifeway.com*; or visit the LifeWay Christian Store serving you.

Printed in the United States of America.

Adult Ministry Publishing
LifeWay Church Resources
One LifeWay Plaza
Nashville, Tennessee 37234-0102

Table of Contents

6   PART 1: **A Biblical Worldview**

7   **CHAPTER 1:** A Christian Worldview: Your View of the World Matters

19   **CHAPTER 2:** The Glory of God: Man-Centered vs. God-Centered Living

31   **CHAPTER 3:** The Bible (Part 1): How Did We Get the Bible?

43   **CHAPTER 4:** The Bible (Part 2): Can We Trust the Bible?

55   **CHAPTER 5:** One Among Many? Christianity Is Unique Among the Religions

68   PART 2: **The Big Questions**

69   **CHAPTER 6:** The Meaning of Life: Does Life Have Meaning Without God?

81   **CHAPTER 7:** The Character of God: Is God Good?

93   **CHAPTER 8:** Suffering: Why Do We Suffer?

105   **CHAPTER 9:** Hell: Is Hell Real and Necessary?

118   PART 3: **The Big Debates**

119   **CHAPTER 10:** Holy Sexuality: Sexuality as God's Good Gift

131   **CHAPTER 11:** Marriage: A God's-Eye View of Marriage

143   **CHAPTER 12:** Human Life: The Sacredness of Human Life

155   **CHAPTER 13:** Christian Care: Concern for Others and the World

Writers

Matt Chandler lead pastor of The Village Church in Dallas, Texas

Marty Duren social media strategist at LifeWay in Nashville, Tennessee

Christian George professor of religious education at Oklahoma Baptist University in Shawnee, Oklahoma

J. D. Greear lead pastor of The Summit Church in Raleigh-Durham, North Carolina

Adam Harwood professor of theology at New Orleans Baptist Theological Seminary in Louisiana

Michael Kelley director of discipleship at LifeWay in Nashville, Tennessee

Philip Nation adult publishing director at LifeWay and teaching pastor of The Fellowship in Mt. Juliet, Tennessee

Mary Jo Sharp professor of apologetics at Houston Baptist University in Texas

Trevin Wax managing editor of *The Gospel Project* at LifeWay in Nashville, Tennessee

Keith Whitfield professor of theology at Southeastern Baptist Theological Seminary in Wake Forest

Jarvis Williams professor at The Southern Baptist Theological Seminary in Louisville, Kentucky

Afshin Ziafat lead pastor of Providence Church in Frisco, Texas

The Gospel Project

Introduction

Some people see the Bible as a collection of stories with morals for life application. But it is so much more. Sure, the Bible has some stories in it, but it is also full of poetry, history, codes of law and civilization, songs, prophecy, letters—even a love letter. When you tie it all together, something remarkable happens. A story is revealed. One story. The story of redemption through Jesus. **This is** *The Gospel Project*.

When we begin to see the Bible as the story of redemption through Jesus Christ, God's plan to rescue the world from sin and death, our perspective changes. We no longer look primarily for what the Bible says about us but instead see what it tells us about God and what He has done. After all, it is the gospel that saves us, and when we encounter Jesus in the pages of Scripture, the gospel works on us, transforming us into His image. **We become God's gospel project.**

Core Values

Deep, but Not Dry

We believe it's best to expect a lot out of those who attend a small group. We don't need to go only as deep as the least knowledgeable person in the group. We may have to "cut up the meat" for new believers and make sure the truth is accessible, but the important thing is that everyone has been fed and is sufficiently nourished.

Christ-Centered

God is the primary Actor in the grand narrative of Scripture, and the gospel of Jesus Christ is the climax of this story. We approach the Old Testament as Jesus did: all the Scriptures testify to Him. We approach New Testament ethics and commands as implications that flow from the gospel—Christ crucified and raised.

Story-Focused

Being Christ-centered naturally brings our focus to the overarching story that the Bible tells in four parts: Creation / Fall / Redemption / Restoration. This helps us connect the dots in the great story that tells the truth about our world and provides a hope-filled outlook on our world because of the future God has promised.

Mission-Driven

Telling the story of the Bible is impossible without leading to mission, as the gospel reveals the heart of our missionary God and His desire to save people of every tribe, tongue, and nation. Keeping a focus on how the gospel leads us to mission is a crucial aspect of how we apply the Bible to our lives.

Part 1

A BIBLICAL WORLDVIEW

How you look at the world matters. It affects what you believe and what you do. Since God created the world and did so with purpose, a God-centered worldview is necessary. Such a worldview focuses on the glory of God as the purpose for the creation, is informed by the Bible as God's Word to us, and recognizes Jesus Christ, God's Son, as the way, the truth, and the life.

Chapter 1

By Trevin Wax

A Christian Worldview

Your View of the World Matters

VOICES FROM *Church History*

"I believe in Christianity as I believe that the Sun has risen, not only because I see it, but because by it I see everything else." [1]
–C. S. Lewis (1898-1963)

VOICES FROM *the Church*

"Apart from a Christian mind we will either be taken captive by the myriad of worldviews contending for our attention, or we will fail to make the Christian voice heard and considered above the din." [2]
–James Emery White

I can't forget the shoes. Piles and piles of them filling the room. Of all the gruesome images I saw at the Holocaust Museum in Washington, DC, the room filled with shoes from Jewish victims is the one thing I can't forget. I think about the people who once owned those shoes, and I mourn the human lives that were lost in a vortex of unspeakable evil.

The tragedy of the Holocaust reminds me of something I heard as a high school student—Ideas have consequences. Adolf Hitler did not come out of nowhere. Before there was the Holocaust, there were decades of philosophical theories advocating superior races, nationalistic laws, and the use of eugenics to weed out inferior peoples. Throw in a dash of "survival of the fittest" from Darwinism and perhaps the pursuit of raw power from Nihilism and eventually we arrive in the concentration camp—a horrifying concoction of various falsehoods.

Ideas do indeed have consequences. But sometimes those consequences are beautiful, as in the early days of Christianity when plagues would sweep through cities in the Roman Empire. While many Roman citizens chose to abandon family and friends and flee the city to escape contamination, early Christians stayed behind to nurse the sick. Because of their belief in a Savior who sacrificed Himself for others, they were content to give their lives as well.

Capitalism. Socialism. Postmodernism. Consumerism. Relativism. Pluralism. There are all sorts of -isms in our world, each representing a different outlook on humanity, each with different opinions about the way societies should function and people should behave. At the beginning, each of these began with an idea.

Some Christians shrug off any effort to study philosophies and "isms." They say things like, "I don't worry myself with what other people think about the world. I just read my Bible and try to do what it says." This line of thinking sounds humble and restrained, but it is far from the mentality of a missionary. If we are to be biblical Christians, we must read the Bible in order to read the culture. As a sent people, it's important to evaluate the -isms of this world in light of God's unchanging revelation. In other words, we read the Bible first so we know how to read world news second.

We also read the Bible in order to know how to engage people around us with the gospel. To be a good missionary, we need to have our own minds formed by the Scriptures, and at the same time, we need to understand how people think—the people we've been called to reach. That's why we need to be familiar with the big questions of life and the big debates in our world.

A worldview is the lens through which we look at the world. At the center of our worldview are the ultimate beliefs we hold, foundational convictions that seem so obvious to us that we don't think much about them. We all have a view of the world. So do the people around us, even if they've never given much thought to it.

I have terrible eyesight and have worn glasses since I was in the first grade. Every morning, I put contact lenses into my eyes so I can see clearly. A worldview is like a contact lens. It's the way we view the world. I don't give a lot of thought to my contacts throughout the day. I don't look at them when they're in my eyes. I look through them and see the world. Worldviews are similar. We look through them and interpret the world around us.

In this chapter, we will see why it is important to think as Christians. Our minds must be transformed and renewed by the power of the gospel. A Christian worldview matters because it sets us apart from unbelievers, helps us progress spiritually, and gives us wisdom to make decisions as believers in Christ. Worldviews matter because people matter. If we are to fulfill our role as Christ's ambassadors, we must be equipped to meet people where they are and to communicate the gospel in a way they can understand.

A Christian worldview matters because it sets us apart from the world (Rom. 12:1-2).

"Christians must be different from the world." Whenever we hear this statement in sermons or read it in books, we usually think about our behavior, right? We nod our heads and think, Yes, our actions must set us apart!

But there's another application of this statement that is equally important. Christians must be different from the world in the way we think. Our thinking must also set us apart. Yes, our actions ought to make us stand out from the world. But at an even deeper level, our thought processes should be different as well because actions follow thoughts.

Let's take a look at Romans 12:1-2, a turning point in the apostle Paul's Letter to the Romans. In these verses, Paul shifted to the letter's final section of careful application. Watch how this unfolds.

1 *Therefore, brothers, by the mercies of God, I urge you to present your bodies as a living sacrifice, holy and pleasing to God; this is your spiritual worship.* 2 *Do not be conformed to this age, but be transformed by the renewing of your mind, so that you may discern what is the good, pleasing, and perfect will of God.*

Do you see the word "therefore" in the beginning of this passage? That word should always remind us to look back to what the writer has been saying. In the previous chapters in Romans, we see how Paul traced the plan of God to redeem the world—beginning with creation, God's promise to Abraham, and then God's provision of salvation through the death and resurrection of Jesus. Paul's view of the world was radically God-centered. This is especially clear in the verses at the end of chapter 11, where he interrupted his letter with a hymn of praise for "the depth of the riches both of the wisdom and the knowledge of God!"

In chapter 12, Paul launched into specific instructions about how to live. In other words, in light of all that has gone before, in light of God's promises and the salvation He has provided through His Son, "present your bodies as a living sacrifice."

You may be thinking, Bodies? Aren't we talking about worldviews? Our minds? Yes, we are. And notice how spiritual transformation includes both. In verse 1, Paul wrote that we must offer our bodies. In verse 2, he wrote that we must be transformed by the renewing of our mind. Mind and matter. Physical and immaterial. Thinking and behavior. Paul didn't just say, "Think rightly." Neither did he simply say, "Behave rightly." Paul knew the gospel transforms both our thoughts and our actions.

If we are to keep from being conformed to this age, we've got to understand the connection between thoughts and deeds. Paul connected them, and so should we.

What does it look like to be conformed to this age? To think in a worldly fashion? The Bible has the answers. It shows us not only what a Christian worldview looks like but also wrong worldviews and how they lead us astray.

Remember the story of Job in the Old Testament? In the Book of Job, we see how a false worldview results in false comfort. Job was a righteous man who went through a severe trial. Along the way, he was "comforted" by his friends, each of whom accused Job of having sinned. Job's friends had a worldview that said, "Everything happens because of cause and effect. Do bad things and bad things will happen to you. Do good things and good things will happen to you." This worldview was the lens through which they viewed Job's suffering. The Book of Job challenges this perspective in light of an all-powerful, all-wise God who permits things to happen that are beyond our understanding.

Consider the Book of Ecclesiastes in the Old Testament. Much of this book expresses the worldview of "life under the sun," a life without meaning and purpose in the face of death. The author does end the book with an affirmation of a biblical worldview, but much of the poetry is written with the perspective that all we can look forward to is death. Though he had amassed great wealth and power, the author knew everything was indeed meaningless apart from the existence of God. And in reflecting on "life under the sun," he wrote a book that helps us understand the mind-set and worldview of someone who lives as though this life is all there is.

Or consider the apostle Paul's lengthy discourse on the resurrection of Christ in 1 Corinthians 15. "If the dead are not raised, let us eat and drink, for tomorrow we die." he wrote in verse 32. In other words, a life of hedonism—the pursuit of pleasure—is acceptable unless the claims at the center of Christianity are true. If Christ has been raised, then there is something more important than immediate pleasure and comfort. Paul contrasted a hedonistic philosophy with Christianity.

The Bible consistently presents a Christian view of the world. Along the way, the biblical authors interacted with and contradicted unbiblical worldviews. We ought to be skilled in doing the same. Developing a Christian worldview will keep us from being conformed to this world.

There is a missional orientation to our nonconformity. Worldviews matter because people matter. Seeking to understand someone with whom we disagree is a way of loving our neighbor. It doesn't mean we accept every point of view as valid, right, or helpful. Neither does it mean we paper over our differences. We must never conform. But it does mean that we will listen and learn like missionaries seeking to understand the culture we are trying to reach. If we are to "present [our] bodies as a living sacrifice," we must live in light of the mercies of God, understand our role in the world as Christ's ambassadors, and answer His call to bear witness to Him and His work.

A Christian worldview matters because it aids our spiritual transformation (Rom. 12:2a).

A Christian worldview is important because it sets us apart from the world. But there's another reason why a Christian worldview matters. Thinking as a Christian is part of the process of sanctification (being made holy). It is an important part of embracing our new identity in Christ. Notice Romans 12:2:

2a *Do not be conformed to this age, but be transformed by the renewing of your mind,*

This verse points us back to chapter 1 of Romans, where Paul laid out the dire situation of humanity before a holy God. There he wrote: "For though they knew God, they did not glorify Him as God or show gratitude. Instead, their thinking became nonsense, and their senseless minds were darkened. Claiming to be wise, they became fools…They exchanged the truth of God for a lie" (Rom. 1:21-22,25).

Romans 1 shows us what happens when we exchange the truth of God for lies. Our minds are darkened, and then we engage in sinful behavior, as is evidenced in Paul's list of sinful attitudes and actions: greed, envy, murder, sexual immorality, etc. (vv. 29-31).

But here in Romans 12, the situation is gloriously reversed! Because of Christ's work, our minds are being renewed. No longer are we senseless sinners living in the dark. Instead, we are redeemed people living in the light of Christ's resurrection. We also live in the light of His regenerating work in our hearts. Through the Spirit, God is at work changing us, conforming us—not to the world but into the image of His Son. By the mercies of God, we have been given a new identity.

Over thirty years ago, a schoolteacher named Jane Elliot conducted an experiment. She told her students that those with brown eyes were smarter than those with blue eyes, and she began giving preferential treatment to brown-eyed students. She put collars on the blue-eyed students to symbolize their inferiority. The results of her experiment showed that the blue-eyed students were affected academically when they had the collars on. They acted in ways that aligned with the identity that had been pronounced over them. [3]

What we think about ourselves matters. What we think about ourselves also affects the way we see the world. That's why thinking as a Christian is a key part of your identity as a follower of Christ. If we have been called the children of God, then surely our new identity should affect the way we think and act.

As a parent, I am proud of my son when I see him growing and maturing. There have been times when, out of a sense of responsibility and love, he has left his toys to go check on his little sister. It warms my heart to see my nine-year-old showing signs of maturity as he grows. In the same way, God is pleased to see our thinking and acting as His children. We bring Him pleasure through our obedience (Rom. 12:2), even though we often falter, stumble, and fall. It's true that we don't always think clearly. Our sanctification is indeed a process, and it is still incomplete. Yet God delights in seeing His children love Him with their minds. He loves to see us embrace the new identity He has given us.

Worldviews provide answers to the fundamental questions of life. How did we get here? Why are we here? Who is in control of the world? Where are we going? What has gone wrong with the world? What is the solution? People may not ask these questions consciously, but their unspoken answers will shape the way they live.

Consider the example of a schoolteacher who goes to work every day convinced that the biggest problem in the world is ignorance. Lack of education leads to crime and is the source of human sorrow. If the world's biggest problem is ignorance, what is the solution? Education, of course! Salvation comes through learning.

A Christian teacher, on the other hand, will see that ignorance may contribute to human suffering, but it's not the ultimate cause. According to the Bible, human sorrow comes from sin—our rebellion against God. Sin is the big problem, and salvation through Christ's atoning death and resurrection is the solution. At the end of the day, the solution is Jesus, not more education.

Can you see the difference? The answers to these worldview questions lead to a different outlook on life. The way you diagnose the world's problem necessarily affects what you believe to be the solution. That's why it's important to have our minds renewed by the power of the Spirit as we study the Scriptures together. We must see the world through the eyes of biblical revelation.

The psalmist wrote, "The revelation of Your words brings light and gives understanding to the inexperienced" (Ps. 119:130). Ultimately, if we have understanding, it's not just because we have attained a natural level of maturity but because we've benefited from God's revelation. Being transformed by the renewing of your mind won't happen apart from God's Spirit working through God's Word. We need the Spirit to illuminate the meaning of the Bible so that we are able to find our place in God's great story of redemption.

A Christian worldview matters because it helps us know how to live (Rom. 12:2b).

Do you see how the apostle Paul gave the renewing of our mind a specific purpose? It's not so we can pride ourselves in thinking rightly. Romans 12:2 makes it plain what the purpose of our spiritual transformation is:

12b *so that you may discern what is the good, pleasing, and perfect will of God.*

Remember we mentioned earlier how a worldview is like having contact lenses? What if I were to put on my contact lenses in the morning and then go back to bed and stare at the ceiling? That would be pointless. The purpose of contact lenses is to help me see clearly throughout the day as I go about the tasks that are assigned to me. In the same way, the point of developing a Christian worldview is not so I can go back to bed, comforted by my good vision. The point of seeing is that I then walk in a biblical way, according to my new identity in Christ.

Sometimes Christians wish the Bible were simpler, a quick and easy guide that lays out every step of obedience. To be sure, the Bible has lots of do's and don'ts. But God didn't choose to lay out in detail specific commands for every possible situation we might find ourselves in.

What the Bible does give us is a grand narrative that focuses our attention on Jesus Christ and His gospel. In this story of redemption, we glean principles for living according to our new identity in Christ. Once we understand our general role in the plan and providence of God, we are called to exercise biblical wisdom in our everyday decisions.

God left us with something better than a simple list of commands. He gave us a renewed mind that—through the power of His Spirit—will be able to discern what actions we should take. He is seeking to transform us so that we can determine God's will in particular situations where explicit instructions are not spelled out in Scripture.

Knowing how to apply the Bible in specific situations is one of the goals of developing a Christian worldview. We see an example of this in 1 Chronicles 12, where we find a list of King David's supporters. As the author listed the soldiers, he wrote of one tribe, "From the Issacharites, who understood the times and knew what Israel should do" (v. 32). In the context of this passage, this tribe's understanding was that David should be made king over all Israel. They knew what Israel should do because they understood the times and who was the rightful king.

In a similar way, we as Christians must understand the times in order to know what to do. We believe Jesus is the rightful King over all the world. And this truth necessarily influences our actions. A Christian worldview is developed in light of who God is and what He has done to reconcile the world to Himself.

Conclusion

What does it mean to live according to our new identity in Christ? First, we must demolish strongholds and false ideas as we cast down the idols we make of ourselves (2 Cor. 10:4-5). Then, in ongoing repentance and faith, we seek to view the world through biblical eyes. We are the citizens of Christ's kingdom. We are those who have been reborn by His Spirit and are inching ever so slowly toward maturity, driven by our hope of the final resurrection.

The more we think as Christians, the more we will have the heart of Christ. That's why we are called to summon others on behalf of the King.

Devotions

SET YOUR MINDS

"Set your minds on what is above, not on what is on the earth," Paul wrote in Colossians 3:2. Many Christians interpret this verse to mean that Christians should always think about spiritual rather than temporal things. But Paul's counsel here certainly can't mean that temporal, physical things are bad and unworthy of attention. After all, the great Christian hope is that we will inhabit a new heavens and a new earth with resurrected, glorified bodies. So what does this verse mean?

Simply put, this is a different way of expressing what Paul wrote in Romans 12:2—"Do not be conformed to this age, but be transformed by the renewing of your mind." In other words, if we have been raised with Christ, we ought to look at the world in light of His reign. Those who have no hope in Christ can't help but view this world as being ultimate. But we who know Jesus are able to put this world in proper perspective. Far from being so heavenly minded that we are of no earthly good, we seek to be heavenly minded in order to be of earthly good.

C. S. Lewis once wrote: "If you read history you will find that the Christians who did most for the present world were just those who thought most of the next…It is since Christians have largely ceased to think of the other world that they have become so ineffective in this."[4] He was right. When we set our minds on what is above, we are given a proper perspective of what is on earth.

Pause and Reflect

1   How often do you think about your future hope as a Christian?

- -

2   How does your future hope affect the way you make decisions?

- -

3   What are some practical ways you can set your mind on what is above today?

OVERCOME WITH AWE

After spending 11 chapters magnifying the grace of God shown to us in Jesus Christ, the apostle Paul broke out into a hymn of praise: "Oh, the depth of the riches both of the wisdom and the knowledge of God! How unsearchable His judgments and untraceable His ways!" (Rom. 11:33).

Have you come to this place before? A place of awe before an all-knowing, all-wise God? Whenever we study the big questions of life, the big debates of our world, and the development of a biblical worldview, we can easily become smug and confident in what we know. We put God in a box and assume we have figured out His ways and His plans.

Reacting against this arrogant overconfidence, some Christians make everything about the Scriptures a mystery. They wonder whether we can know anything with certainty about who God is and what He has done.

The apostle Paul struck the right balance. Paul believed he knew things about God, and he held these truths with confidence. At the same time, the more Paul knew, the more he realized he didn't know everything. In other words, though Paul could know many things about God with absolute certainty, he understood that he didn't know God exhaustively.

So what was Paul's response? He bowed his knees in worship. He proclaimed what he knew about God based on God's revelation of Himself, and then he knelt in worship, fully recognizing his own limitations of knowledge. That's where intellectual growth should lead us, not to overconfidence in our ability to figure God out but to our knees in worship, in awe of His goodness to us.

Pause and Reflect

1   What is the role of worship in developing a Christian worldview?

---

2   What are some ways you can turn your knowledge of God into more opportunities for worship?

---

3   Praise God for some of His attributes described in the Scriptures.

Turn Your Eyes upon Jesus

In 1922, Helen Lemmel composed the popular hymn "Turn Your Eyes upon Jesus." The refrain includes these lyrics: "Turn your eyes upon Jesus, Look full in His wonderful face, And the things of earth will grow strangely dim In the light of His glory and grace." There's certainly something to be said for these words, particularly the truth that all the glories of earth pale in comparison to Christ's glory. Understood this way, the lyrics are spot on.

But there is something about the lyrics to this song that could be misleading. The line about the things of earth growing strangely dim could lead someone to think that everything earthly fades away when we turn our eyes to Jesus. Not so. Instead, when we turn our eyes upon Jesus, the things of earth ought to grow strangely clearer. In other words, looking at Jesus ought to help us see the earth better—as it truly is. Far from disappearing from view, earthly things come into clearer and sharper focus when we turn our eyes upon Jesus.

A Christian worldview ought to lift the hazy fog from our eyes so that we see this world from a biblical perspective. When we turn our eyes upon Jesus, we ought to see the rest of the world in sharper focus. We are given the ability to understand how ideas and actions differ from Jesus' vision.

So, by all means, let's keep our eyes on Jesus. But not so we can escape from this earthly reality, but so we can interpret it rightly, in light of His glory and grace.

Pause and Reflect

1 What are some practical ways to "turn your eyes upon Jesus"?

---

2 How does our faith in Jesus as Lord over all help us understand the world around us?

---

3 What are some personal convictions you hold that are directly attributable to your faith in Jesus?

DISCUSSION QUESTIONS

1   What is one significant idea of our time that has had far-reaching implications? How do we determine whether or not these ideas and consequences are right or wrong?

2   What consequences that might flow from the following ideas: (1) Morality is determined by the consensus of a society. (2) Religion deals with private spirituality, not public policy. (3) The right thing to do is always relative to a person's situation.

3   What experiences in your life have impacted your worldview? Did they alter your ultimate beliefs? If so, how? If not, why not? What are some biblical teachings that have challenged and changed your worldview?

4   In your experience, has Christian teaching primarily focused on right thinking or right behavior? What happens when we focus on one to the exclusion of the other?

5   How can we be more aware of the worldviews of people around us? How can we lovingly but boldly live in a way that refuses to conform to the world's pattern of thinking?

6   In what ways does our understanding of who we are in Christ affect our actions? What do we communicate to the world when we claim one identity but live out another?

7   What are some answers provided by other religions to foundational worldview questions? How do Christianity's answers differ?

8   What role does the Holy Spirit play in helping us understand our actions in light of the Bible's teaching? Why is it important to understand the worldview of the Bible as we make decisions?

9   What are some negative ways our mission is affected when false worldviews infiltrate our thinking?

10 What are some ways parents can train their children to think biblically? How can church members encourage one another toward biblical thinking?

Chapter 2

By Philip Nation

The Glory of God

Man-Centered vs. God-Centered Living

VOICES FROM *Church History*

"The deepest passion of the heart of Jesus was not the saving of men, but the glory of God; and then the saving of men, because that is for the glory of God." [1]
–G. Campbell Morgan (1863-1945)

VOICES FROM *the Church*

"What are you really living for? It's crucial to realize that you either glorify God or you glorify something or someone else. You're always making something look big." [2]
–Ken Sande

What is the center of the universe? Whenever we consider our lives—our universe—we usually find a center point around which everything revolves. It could be a relationship, our marriage, children, a job, a dream, science, a favorite sports team, an idea, or a religious philosophy. The center of our universe can be something of grave importance or utter silliness according to the rest of humanity.

It probably goes without saying that most people place "self" at the center of their personal universe. We do so by default. It is, after all, our nature to be selfish. But the big question is this: Does the center of your life line up with what is at the center of the universe? Does *your* center line up with *the* center?

The Scriptures point to God as the center of the universe. The Bible reveals truth about God first and then mankind. Moving throughout the totality of the Bible, we see that not only are the Scriptures centered upon God but all of creation revolves around Him as well. In order to have a biblical view of the world, we must recognize that God is at the center of the Bible and the world.

There is a phrase we use to help us understand God's center point in all of creation—*the glory of God.*

As Christians, we know the glory of God should be the reason for how we live, what we do as the church, and why we care for others. When someone feeds the hungry, it is for the glory of God. When a well is dug for the poor in Haiti, it's for God's glory. We build cathedrals, rock babies in a preschool ministry, and hang out with friends—all for the glory of God. We plant churches, witness to unbelievers, and send missionaries around the globe for the glory of God.

We know the glory of God is important, but we often have a difficult time defining the concept. Can you tell me what it is? What exactly is the glory of God? Let's find out together.

In this chapter, we will contrast a man-centered view of the world with a God-centered view of the world by taking a close look at the glory of God. We will see that the glory of God refers to God's manifest work, His excellent reputation, and His inherent beauty. Then we will look at how the glory of God impacts our lives today and fuels our mission as Christ's ambassadors.

What is the glory of God? (Ex. 33:19-23; 34:5-9)

A lot happens in the Book of Exodus. Within these pages, we see how God heard the cries of His people enslaved by the Egyptians. We watch Him perform numerous miracles to deliver them to a new land prepared just for them. We also see God's people doubt God's goodness and then be consigned to wander through the desert for 40 years.

Shortly after the Israelites' deliverance from Egypt, God called Moses to the pinnacle of Mount Sinai in order to receive the law. While on the mountain,

Moses begged for God's presence to remain with His people. And God promised His presence.

We don't know what Moses was feeling: giddy with the answer, energized by the experience on the mountain, or just bold because of God's agreement to stay with the people. No matter the reason, Moses suddenly asked for what seems to be an impossible request: "Please, let me see Your glory" (Ex. 33:18).

As I read this passage, I want to say, "What!? Are you crazy? You can't ask for that. Ask for help. Ask for direction. Ask to know God's will. But you don't ask to see God's glory." Instinct says that a person simply cannot survive such an encounter. And those instincts are right!

Let's see how God answered Moses' request:

19 *He said, "I will cause all My goodness to pass in front of you, and I will proclaim the name Yahweh before you. I will be gracious to whom I will be gracious, and I will have compassion on whom I will have compassion."* 20 *But He answered, "You cannot see My face, for no one can see Me and live."* 21 *The* LORD *said, "Here is a place near Me. You are to stand on the rock,* 22 *and when My glory passes by, I will put you in the crevice of the rock and cover you with My hand until I have passed by.* 23 *Then I will take My hand away, and you will see My back, but My face will not be seen."*

Moses was allowed to see the trailing end of God's being. But God's face was off limits to human perception. Whatever God's face looks like must be too much for us to bear. We don't know why or how, but His beauty and power must be so brilliant it would simply short-circuit a human. If we saw God's face, we would die. Moses was asking for something that would kill him—and I think he knew it. But wouldn't we all make the sacrifice if only for a moment we could catch a glimpse of the face of God?

And so the story unfolds. Moses was placed safely in a crevice as God passed by. But God protected Moses with His own hand. In the next chapter, we see the event and Moses' reaction. Take a look:

5 *The* LORD *came down in a cloud, stood with him there, and proclaimed His name Yahweh.* 6 *Then the* LORD *passed in front of him and proclaimed: Yahweh—Yahweh is a compassionate and gracious God, slow to anger and rich in faithful love and truth,* 7 *maintaining faithful love to a thousand generations, forgiving wrongdoing, rebellion, and sin. But He will not leave the guilty unpunished, bringing the consequences of the fathers' wrongdoing on the children and grandchildren to the third and fourth generation.*

8 Moses immediately bowed down to the ground and worshiped. 9 Then he said, "My Lord, if I have indeed found favor in Your sight, my Lord, please go with us. Even though this is a stiff-necked people, forgive our wrongdoing and sin, and accept us as Your own possession."

When Moses asked to witness God's glory, the Lord gave an odd answer. He said, "I will cause all My goodness to pass in front of you, and I will proclaim the name Yahweh before you. I will be gracious to whom I will be gracious, and I will have compassion on whom I will have compassion" (Ex. 33:19). Moses asked to see God's glory, but God described something different than what we expect. Still, in His answer I believe we find a description of God's glory. It can be understood in three points.

Manifest Work

First, God's glory is found in His character. It is the physical representation of God's perfect character. When Moses asked to see God's glory, the Lord's response was to cause all His goodness to pass in front of him (Ex. 33:19). But goodness as a character trait cannot be seen unless it is expressed. God's glory is defined in His manifest work. It is the representation of His character through His activity.

When we want to know about God's glory, we often try to picture something intangible. But God's goodness is not an ethereal light. It is rooted in reality. God's glory and goodness is worked out in the life of eternity and in the dirt of earth. Glory is made known in the manifest work of God.

In the story continuing from Exodus 33 to 34, a primary focus is on God's character as it relates to compassion and forgiveness. The glory of God is most easily distinguished for us through His work. It is tangible. In Exodus 34:6-7, the Lord indicated that His glory is expressed through His love and justice. The work of God is the expression of God's character through His perfect execution of love and truth. We experience God's glory in every activity of His work.

Excellent Reputation

The second description of God's glory is in the proclamation of His name. In the ancient world, a man's name held great meaning. Even today, in Eastern cultures, people are often given a name that signifies something of their family lineage or their parents' hope for the person they will become. In a word or two, a person's name represents one's public reputation.

At the request by Moses to reveal His glory, God passed by the place where Moses was hidden and declared something specific—His name. In Exodus 34:5, God spoke the name "Yahweh" as He passed by. It was the description of His own self to Moses.

I was named after my father. I am Philip W. Nation II. Curiously, Mom and Dad did not name me Philip W. Nation, Junior. Why? Because they never wanted anyone to call me "Junior." They wanted me simply to be "Phil." Despite their efforts, I became known as "Little Phil." You see, my father is 6' 2" and a strapping 210 pounds. On the other hand, I am 5' 8" and (let's say for the sake of fun) a strapping 165 pounds. It was not until I entered college that I was able to shed "Little Phil" and become "Philip." Since earning my doctorate, I now only have to fight against the occasional joke by a church member calling me "Dr. Phil." (Everybody gets one, and only one, shot at it.)

My wife, Angie, and I have two sons, and we named them with specific reasons. Our oldest is Andrew Timothy, meaning "the strong one who honors God." Our youngest is Christopher Sage, meaning "with Christ inside, the wise one." You may wonder, *Why put so much into the meaning of their names?* The answer is simple—we hope that their character will grow to reflect their names.

Names are normally just that—a name, a moniker, the word you call something. But God's name expresses something of His glory. The name Yahweh is a derivative of the Hebrew verb "to be." In its essence, by attributing this name to Himself, God was expressing the idea that He is self-existent. In other words, no one and nothing else created Him or caused Him to come into being. Yahweh is eternal by His own power.

The name communicates that God's glory is eternal, His power is self-sustaining, and He is everlasting. The name Yahweh sets Him apart from all of the false gods of our own imaginations and the weaknesses of this world.

Inherent Beauty

When I was a teenager, *The Clash of the Titans* was a blockbuster movie filled with cheesy action sequences, an implausible story line, "state of the art" special effects, and overwhelming odds for the hero. If you know the story line, the hero had to overcome the capricious whims of the mythical Greek gods. The scenes I remember best are those of Zeus and the rest of the Greek pantheon gathered on Mount Olympus. The directors must have opened the iris of every camera. The special effect team added in as much brightness and rays of light as digitally possible. It was a scene of almost painful light.

Bright light is what most people think about when they consider the phrase *the glory of God*. It is the idea that God is clothed in unbearable brightness in heaven's throne room. To some extent, that view of God's glory has some merit.

In Exodus 33:20, God said to Moses, "You cannot see My face, for no one can see Me and live." It was the intention of God to show up in front of the mountain. In His kindness, God wanted Moses to experience His glory without it overtaking his life. The full force of God's beauty is apparently too much for a person to survive.

The glory of God cannot be witnessed unless God is actually present. His inherent beauty is the radiant manifestation of God's attributes and actions. Therefore, He shows up. Glory is not just an ideal. It is found in God's arrival, in His presence.

God commanded Moses to hide in a crevice on the side of the mountain. Even then, God personally obscured Moses' sight of His glory so it would not kill him. God's presence must be so blindingly perfect that a man can only stand to look at the trailing end of it passing by. Still, the face of Moses was left glowing from the experience. God has an inherent beauty that is gloriously overwhelming.

Another passage that speaks to the grandeur of God's glory is Ezekiel 1. The chapter is a lengthy description of the vision God gave Ezekiel regarding His glory. Reacting to it, Ezekiel said, "This was the appearance of the form of the LORD's glory. When I saw it, I fell facedown and heard a voice speaking" (Ezek. 1:28). A similar vision was given to John in his writing of the Book of Revelation to conclude the New Testament. In both visions, the beauty of God is the centerpiece. By it, Yahweh communicates who He is and the glory He possesses.

Our identity and God's glory (2 Cor. 3:12-18)

God's glory matters—not only for God but also for who we are in Christ. The apostle Paul often used the phrase "in Christ" to describe who we are and how we are to live. Our salvation has its origination and completion in Jesus the Christ. That's why it's not enough to think about God's glory in general. We've got to look at God's glory in Christ in order to gain a proper understanding of our identity.

In John 17, we find the longest recorded prayer of Jesus. Jesus prayed in the first verse: "Father, the hour has come. Glorify Your Son so that the Son may glorify You." And in verse 5: "Now, Father, glorify Me in Your presence with that glory I had with You before the world existed."

As Jesus concluded the prayer, He prayed for all those who would become Christians after the apostles: "I have given them the glory You have given Me. May they be one as We are one" (v. 22).

Christ has given us an unfathomable gift. From Jesus we receive the glory of God that He personally shares with His Father! This gift is rooted in love (v. 24) and results in unity (v. 22).

Let's take a look at something similar written by the apostle Paul in 2 Corinthians 3:12-18:

12 *Therefore, having such a hope, we use great boldness.* 13 *We are not like Moses, who used to put a veil over his face so that the Israelites could not stare at the end of what was fading away,* 14 *but their minds were closed. For to this day, at the reading of the old covenant, the same veil remains; it is not lifted, because it is set aside only in Christ.* 15 *Even to this day, whenever Moses is read, a veil lies over their hearts,* 16 *but whenever a person turns to the Lord, the veil is removed.* 17 *Now the Lord is the Spirit, and where the Spirit of the Lord is, there is freedom.* 18 *We all, with unveiled faces, are looking as in a mirror at the glory of the Lord and are being transformed into the same image from glory to glory; this is from the Lord who is the Spirit.*

This passage takes us back to Moses' experience after meeting God on the mountain. Upon his arrival back at the camp of the Israelites, they begged him to cover his face because they could not stomach the sight of a man awash with God's glory. Moses acquiesced and the effect began to dissipate. Fear of God's holiness among the Israelites mitigated their experience of God's glory.

In his letter to the Corinthian church, Paul taught that when a person moves from the law to the grace of Christ, the veil is removed. Through faith, they can fully see and experience the effects of God's reputation in action, of His work on their behalf, and of His beauty in their lives. Even more, they become a mirror for others to see God's glory as well. The glory of God at work in the life of a Christian brings freedom (v. 17).

Our identity is now different. Before, we were spiritually blind. Now, we are mirrors for the radiance of God. Before, we were dead in sin. Now, we are being transformed into the image of Christ (v. 18). Believers need to understand the glory of God so we can understand our identity in Christ. He shares His being with the Father and now shares Their glory with us.

It is often said that a couple that has been married for years begins to look like one another in the way they dress and present themselves. They don't try to make these changes, but they are transformed by the presence of the other. That is not unlike what is happening to believers who live in God's presence. Paul described us as reflecting the glory of the Lord and being transformed into the same image, from glory to glory.

When Moses stood in the presence of God, he was transformed. His face would start to shine like the sun, but when he went down Mount Sinai, he would cover the brightness with a veil. Paul tells us here that Moses hid his face because that glory was not lasting. It would fade away (v. 13).

But that is not the case for believers. We who have been given the Spirit of God and can see "the light of the gospel of the glory of Christ" (4:4) can always be in the presence of God in worship and prayer and always have Christ within us. When we turn to the Lord, we reflect His glory, not in a transitory way as did Moses but eternally, like Christ Himself. And we are transformed by it.

As one writer states: "Like the old couple who has begun to look like one another, as we spend time in the presence of God we are slowly transformed. We begin to look more and more like Christ, moving from one stage of glory to the next. We do not change by our own efforts, but simply by turning our eyes to Jesus."[3]

Conclusion

The glory of God isn't just an idea in a book on the shelf. It matters on Tuesday morning when you are on the assembly line, in a staff meeting, or making a sales pitch. Because God has graciously moved us from being a slave to the law to a child in His family, we are reflectors of His glory. You can search the entire Bible and will find that there are no exception clauses as to when the reflecting is done. If you are in Christ, you are a mirror, an ambassador, a carrier of God's glory.

So what is your response to this incredible news? It could be one of shame. We know our sin and can mope about thinking about how unworthy we are. And you would be right and wrong. We are unworthy, yes, but Christ has clothed us in His righteousness making us worthy.

The glory of God should instead give us a God-centered perspective and God-centered priorities. Living by and for God's glory causes us to see life's circumstances and the people around us through the lens of eternity. Difficult circumstances are not temporary interruptions to our lives but potential platforms and scenery for God's glory to shine through us.

Joining the mission of God to display His glory for all to see and respond to must become the highest priority. After all, it is God's. God deserves our response to His glory to be absolute. We are the ones who will possibly attribute glory to another—an idol, a pleasure, an idea, or self. Our call, our mission, is to attribute glory to the only One to whom it belongs—Yahweh.

Devotions

FAME

We live in a fame-obsessed culture. Then again, it has probably always been that way. Early in the history of humanity, everyone had disobeyed God's explicit command to scatter and multiply across the land. Instead, they all clustered and hoarded at a city called Babel. Finally, in a bid to once again grasp at the place of divinity, they decided to embark on a ludicrous endeavor—to build a building so high, so grand, and so heavenly that it would make them invincibly famous. Those who settled in Babel wanted to be the superpower of the Earth. In essence, they wanted to replace the Lord as the famous One.

We still suffer from this spiritual disease. The grasp for fame is a sickening sensation. When it is attained, we gain the sense of security for a short while. However, it is addicting. It is necessary to become popular again and again and again. In our culture, we allow people to be famous without any concrete reason. Debutantes appear on a red carpet. The "beautiful people" have their photographs plastered across magazine covers. In general, we have degraded the idea of fame to simply showing up in a party dress at the right event.

Fame, instead, should be recaptured as a tribute to worth and character. The settlers of Babel said they wanted to make a name for themselves. They had a grand accomplishment in mind, but it was more delusional than anything. Their heart's desire was not really in the construction of a palatial tower but in the fame that came from it. They wanted what we commonly and biblically refer to as glory. The desire for self-aggrandizement will always seek to supersede the rightful place of God's fame in our lives.

Pause and Reflect

1   What are the reasons so many people desire fame?

2   How is living for the fame of Christ a tribute to His worth and character?

Glory Thief

In the Book of John, Jesus described Himself as a door, the door to life. The opposite characters to Him in the metaphor were thieves and robbers. In John 10:10 comes an oft-quoted statement, "A thief comes only to steal and to kill and to destroy. I have come so that they may have life and have it in abundance."

Our Lord highlights that whereas He, the King of glory, gives life, our chief Enemy is intent on taking it. The chief glory thief is our Adversary…Lucifer… the Devil…Satan. It has always been his intention to steal away God's glory and thereby steal away our lives. The painful truth is that we are too often the Devil's willing accomplices.

The chief glory thief is the one who would like nothing else than to steal away a person's attention from the One who truly deserves glory, worship, and fame among the nations. As our adversary, Satan wants us to be in a posture of defending *our* sovereignty against God—the One who truly deserves all praise. Our enemy will deceive us into believing that by following his tempting offers of pleasure and fame, we can take our rightful place in the world. Satan wants you to think more about the temporary pleasures and positions in life rather than the eternal glory that belongs to God.

In 1 Peter 5:8, we are warned: "Be serious! Be alert! Your adversary the Devil is prowling around like a roaring lion, looking for anyone he can devour." He has come to kill, not nip at your heels like a declawed house cat. No, he is a fierce predator who seeks to devour you. You must be on your guard, ever vigilant against the chief glory thief.

Pause and Reflect

1 What are some practical ways we can remain alert and vigilant against the chief glory thief?

- -

2 How can we re-center our lives on the eternal glory that belongs to God?

MISSION OF GLORY

In 2 Thessalonians, Paul wrote about the impending judgment that would fall upon all unbelievers. The letter is a strong warning to understand the brevity of history and to live as if the end of all things is quickly approaching. Take a moment to read 2 Thessalonians 2:13-17, where Paul encouraged believers to think about our salvation and what has been afforded to us.

This passage reminds us that through the gospel, we have obtained the glory of Jesus. It is certainly one of the great and mysterious gifts of salvation for which we are utterly unworthy. It is God's great worth that gives Him the right to exclusively hold on to glory. In the gospel, Jesus chooses to share it with us.

We are a people constantly in search of encouragement and a pat on the back at work. We desire to be cheered on by coworkers, fellow classmates, and family members. Our hope is that someone notices our hard work and effort at life's problems and challenges.

But consider the encouragement given to you by the presence of glory. God puts the work of His character into action to guard you from sin's destructive forces. The Lord gives you His name: Christian. We are identified with His reputation and can carry it into the world like Moses carried "I AM" into the presence of Egypt's pharaoh. And God the Holy Spirit indwells us with His beautiful presence. He teaches us the mysteries of the Scriptures, imparts discernment and wisdom for our lives, and empowers us for the mission given to the church.

Pause and Reflect

1   Spend some time thinking of the great privilege it is to know the glory of God.

- -

2   How does the glory of God help break down the barriers that we think hinder our mission?

- -

3   How does the glory of God in our lives help us fight temptation?

DISCUSSION QUESTIONS

1   What are some ways you might discover what is at the center of your life? If someone asked you to explain the glory of God, how would you describe it? What words come to mind?

2   Do most people think of a face-to-face encounter with God as dangerous or do we tend to take God's presence too lightly? Explain your answer.

3   Is there anything about God's response to Moses' request in Exodus 33 that surprises you? How is God's sovereign majesty and His loving kindness on display in His response?

4   List some of God's actions that manifested His glory. Why is it important for us to understand God's glory in action? What do we lose if we only think of God's glory in terms of brightness or distant majesty?

5   What are the dangers of thinking of our reflection of God's glory only in terms of *being* and not *doing*?

6   Think about the name we bear—Christian. What does this name communicate? What should it communicate? In what ways ought our lives be different because of this name?

7   It's been said that the human soul is on a quest to find beauty. Where do people look for beauty and wonder? How do the traces of beauty in our world point us to the Creator?

8   The apostle Paul encouraged Christians to do everything to the glory of God (1 Cor. 10:31). What are some practical ways to obey this command at work? At home? At school?

9   List a number of the spiritual benefits we receive when we put our trust in Christ. Before reading 2 Corinthians 3:12-18, would you have put the gift of receiving glory from Christ on the list? Why or why not?

10 What is the relationship between reflecting God's glory and engaging in His mission? What are some signs of self-centeredness in your life that keep you from reflecting God's glory?

Chapter 3

By Keith Whitfield

The Bible (Part 1)

How Did We Get the Bible?

VOICES FROM *Church History*

"The Bible contains truth found nowhere else. Human reason may discover certain truths about God. But the revealed truth of the Bible exceeds these so as to defy comparison. One may exhaust the meaning of the contents of other books, but not that of the Bible." [1]
–Herschel Hobbs (1907-1995)

VOICES FROM *Church History*

"The Bible is a supernatural, spiritual, sovereign, surviving, sustaining, super-charged book about my Savior." [2]
–Adrian Rogers (1931-2005)

The modern pencil dates back to the 1500s. A simple writing instrument that has stood the test of time! The design is simple: a piece of wood with a small graphite rod in the center, topped with a rubber-like, synthetic eraser.

Have you ever stopped to think about everything that goes into the creation of this 10-cent writing instrument? It starts with someone planting cedar trees, someone else mining graphite, and a chemist in a lab somewhere working out the formula for synthetic rubber. The trees grow. They are cut down, loaded on a truck, and hauled to a sawmill. The cedars are cut into blocks that are then sliced into pieces the width of half a pencil.

After the graphite is removed from the earth, it is ground down to powder and mixed with clay. Water is added, and the mixture is then shaped into long spaghetti-like strings to be dried in a kiln, dipped into wax, and cut to the right size. Finally, the graphite strings are inserted into a cedar plank and another plank glued down to cover the graphite inside the pencil. Then it is topped off with a synthetic piece of rubber.

All that work for a 10-cent writing instrument that school-aged kids use to "pencil fight"—an instrument we sometimes lose or sharpen into nothing!

The Bible is the Word of God, and for those who understand its value, the Word is more precious than pure gold, sweeter than the honey from the comb (Ps. 19:10). It renews one's life and makes the inexperienced wise (Ps. 19:7). It is living and able to cut to the bone, judging thoughts of the heart (Heb. 4:12). Oh, and don't forget this—it endures forever (Isa. 40:8)!

But how did this book that endures forever, with the power to renew your life and judge your very thoughts, get into your hands? How did we get the Bible?

In this chapter, we will examine the way God gave us His Word. First, we will look at the truth of God's inspiration of human authors to write the Scriptures. Second, we will explore the process of canonization—how God's people recognized the authority of His Word. Third, we will see how God has preserved His Word over time that we might hear His voice today and proclaim His gospel to the world.

Inspiration: The Holy Spirit inspired the authors of Scripture in such a way that the words they wrote down are the very Word of God.

"How did we get the Bible?" To answer this question, we need to go back to the Bible's composition. Questions about how the Bible was composed take us, of course, to the Author and the authors—or better said, the Author who inspired the authors.

First, the authors. The Bible was written over a span of 1,500 years. Moses likely recorded Genesis around 1400 B.C. John probably wrote the Book of Revelation late in the first century A.D., around A.D. 90. Over 40 different authors contributed to the Bible. Its 66 books were written from multiple locations by people scattered over three continents.

But what about the Author with a capital *A*? Christians see a remarkable coherence in this library of books. We claim the Bible to be the very Word of God. It is the definitive book for knowing God and His grand purposes in the world. The Bible tells a story—the true story of the whole world.

It's not just Christians who claim the Bible is God's Word. The Bible testifies about itself that it is the inspired Word of God. The apostle Paul made this clear in 2 Timothy 3:

16 *All Scripture is inspired by God and is profitable for teaching, for rebuking, for correcting, for training in righteousness,* 17 *so that the man of God may be complete, equipped for every good work.*

God not only revealed Himself in creation, He chose to reveal Himself in the Person of Jesus Christ and in the written Word that testifies to Christ. How did He give us His Word? Through His work of inspiration.

God inspired the authors of Scripture so that the very words they wrote down were the Word of God. God's inspiration of the Scriptures is described by the apostle Peter in this way: The authors were "moved by" or "carried along by" the Holy Spirit (2 Pet. 1:19-21).

Over time, the idea of biblical inspiration has confused some people. Here are a few inadequate views of *inspiration*:

1. The human authors were inspired in the way we are inspired to create something. You and I might be inspired by a sunset to create a painting. Or perhaps we might refer to a novel as "inspired" or "insightful." But biblical inspiration does not refer to an inspiring work of God in the lives of the human authors that caused them to write inspiring words. We mean something more by *inspiration*.

2. Ordinary human words are transformed into divine speech. Some see inspiration as a matter of God taking ordinary human documents and then transforming them into His Word. But this is not the biblical view of inspiration either.

3. Inspiration refers to the reader, not the author. Others suggest that inspiration refers not to the content of the Bible itself but to the reader of the Bible. God takes normal human words and uses them to "inspire" the reader as he or she reads the Bible. But this is far from the biblical portrait.

None of these are adequate explanations of what Christians mean by *inspiration*. In 2 Timothy 3:16, Paul invented the word that is often translated as "inspired by God." A closer look at this word helps us understand *inspiration*. The word Paul used is actually a combination of two words. The first is "God," and the second literally means "to blow" or "to breathe out."

Therefore, when the text says, "inspired by God," it is referring to a specific action. We get a descriptive picture from this term, a picture that shows Scripture being breathed out, springing forth to us directly from God Himself. Inspiration means that the words themselves are the words God spoke, and the human authors wrote down what God spoke. Paul was saying, "All Scripture is God-breathed."

What does this process of inspiration look like? First, God delivered His message through human authors. They recorded the exact words God spoke to them (Deut. 31:19), which is why we consider inspiration to be verbal.

At the same time, God worked through the personalities of the human writers. That's why Paul could say, "what I write to you is the Lord's command" (1 Cor. 14:37; see also 2 Pet. 1:20-21). Throughout this process, God did not override the freedom and expression of the authors. Instead, He worked through them to inspire the very words He intended to give to His people.

So God directed the authors to write His words, the exact words He purposed to be written, and yet the experiences, perspective, personality, and style of the human authors were preserved. That's why Paul has a distinctive style. Peter doesn't sound like Luke. John writes differently than Matthew. God used the personalities of the human authors in order to get His message across.

There's another picture the word "God-breathed" gives us. In the creation story, God breathed into the nostrils of humanity (an image molded from dirt) and gave Adam life: "Then the LORD God formed the man out of the dust from the ground and breathed the breath of life into his nostrils, and the man became a living being" (Gen. 2:7). Adam's life was God-breathed. The "livingness" and vitality of human life came directly from God Himself.

Now let's return to the picture we see when Paul described the Bible as God-breathed. Because the Scripture is breathed out by God, it has power and vitality. No wonder the writer of Hebrews could say, "For the Word of God is living and effective" (Heb. 4:12)!

Canonization: The Holy Spirit guided the early church to recognize the inspired Word of God.

In addition to inspiration, 2 Timothy 3:16-17 points us to another answer to the question "How did we get the Bible?" While the apostle Paul was not making this point directly, he nevertheless implied that Scripture is different from what is not Scripture. In other words, there is a distinct set of writings considered inspired while other writings are not.

Paul called these writings "Scripture," which means "sacred writings." When Paul referred to "all Scripture," he was pointing to a collection of writings that share specific qualities.

At this point, we should remember that Paul had in mind the Old Testament, although it's possible he may have been referring to some New Testament writings as well. Regardless, whatever collection of books Paul referred to as "Scripture," it is clear they are sacred because they are breathed out by God. Inspiration is the quality that makes the writing sacred. But *canonization* is the next step—recognizing which books are inspired.

"You just don't measure up." Has anyone ever said this to you before? Maybe it was a boss who was letting you go. Maybe it was a parent expressing disappointment in you. Maybe it was the guy at the theme park saying you weren't tall enough for a ride! No one wants to hear these words. Why not? Because the idea behind *measuring up* is an objective standard of some sort and you don't reach it.

The question of *measuring up* brings us to the issue of canonization. You see, just as the Jewish people recognized the books of the Old Testament as sacred Scripture, the Christian church came to recognize the New Testament to be sacred Scripture as well. Over time, the church recognized the 66 books of the Old and New Testaments as the church's *canon.*

A canon is a collection of books received as the authoritative "rule" for faith. The word *canon* comes from the Hebrew word for *reed* and *stalk* (1 Kings 14:15; Job 40:21). In ancient times, reeds were used as a measuring stick—a rule or standard. So, as this word developed, the Greeks began to use the word more broadly as any type of standard or guideline. In Galatians 6:16, Paul used it in this way when he called the cross the "rule" or "standard" for faith.

Around the year A.D. 352, the word *canon* was associated with the authoritative and sacred list of books for the Christian faith. [3] What qualified a book to be included in the canon was not that the church determined it belonged in the collection but that the book had God's authority in what it taught.

The precedent for a canon comes from Scripture itself. Moses wrote the first five books of the Old Testament during the 40 years in the wilderness and presented it to the priests for them to store beside the ark of the covenant in the tabernacle (Deut. 31:9,26). The Israelites revered the Word that Moses recorded (Josh. 8:35). Centuries later, having been ignored in the temple, these books were found by King Josiah (2 Kings 22:3-20). As the history of Israel unfolds, additional books were added to the books of Moses. So we see in Daniel 9:2 the collection of books endured and the Book of Jeremiah had been added to them.

The writing of the Old Testament would not be completed until around 430 B.C. with the Book of Malachi. By 100 B.C., the Septuagint, a Greek translation of the Old Testament, was completed. It became common to reference the Law, Prophets, and Writings as a three-fold division of the Old Testament. Jesus referred to the Old Testament Scriptures by the Law, the Prophets, and the Psalms (Luke 24:44). These facts point to a settled Old Testament canon more than 100 years before Jesus' birth.

By the time Jesus started His ministry, there must have been a settled Old Testament canon. Of all the disputes He had with the Jewish religious leaders over the proper interpretation of the Old Testament, they never debated which books were authoritative. Before the close of the first century A.D., the Jewish historian Josephus referenced a completed canon of Old Testament books.[4]

In the New Testament, the collection of sacred books expands. Paul wrote with awareness that he was writing Scripture (1 Cor. 14:37-38; 1 Thess. 2:13). Peter considered the letters of Paul on par with the rest of Scripture (2 Pet. 3:15-16). John attributed God's authority to the writing of Revelation, with the threat of judgment to those who add to or take away from it (Rev. 22:6-8,18-19).

Before the close of the first century A.D., a number of the early church leaders treated the New Testament books as possessing divine authority for the church. The church continued to affirm the New Testament books as canonical through the first four centuries of the church.

In A.D. 367, a complete list of the New Testament books was provided by Athanasius in a letter to his parishioners.[5] These books were recognized as being divine based on four principles:
1. Was the book written by an apostle or someone recognized as having authority?
2. Does the book agree with the apostolic teaching?
3. Was the book universally accepted by the church?
4. Does the book have a self-authenticating divine nature?

Preservation: The Holy Spirit has providentially preserved God's Word throughout history.

We've used 2 Timothy 3:16-17 as our main text for answering the question "How did we get the Bible?" We've answered this question so far in two ways: claiming that God inspired His Word and recognizing that only certain books have divine authority for what we should believe and how we should live. But we still have to answer how that collection of sacred writings got into our hands and into our language. While we do not have a full history of how the Bible has been transmitted to us in 2 Timothy 3:16-17, this text points us to the theological basis for answering the question.

Consider the function of Scripture, described in verse 17—to prepare all of God's people (from every time and place) to be "complete, equipped for every good work." The Word of God is sufficient for this task. Why? Because it is inspired by the Spirit. Likewise, the Word accomplishes this task by penetrating the hearts of Christians from one generation to the next.

At every point in history, God's Word has been protected for and provided to God's people. The message of God's grand plan of salvation—through the death and resurrection of Jesus Christ—is the same message we have today. As we read our Bibles, the promise of 1 Peter 1:22-25 is being fulfilled. Grass withers and flowers die, but the Word of God will last forever (see Isa. 40:8).

While it does not directly address how the Bible is preserved for all of God's people across time, 2 Timothy 3:16-17 points us to the function of God's Word, which presupposes the truth that God will preserve His Word in order to equip His people to accomplish His mission.

When we hold our English Bibles in our hands, we should recognize that we are the beneficiaries of selfless men and women who committed to preserve God's Word by copying manuscripts, translating it into the common language, and ensuring that God's people would benefit from hearing His voice.

God's providence in preserving the Scriptures is remarkable to consider. The Old Testament was transmitted by a special group of priests, called scribes, who meticulously made new copies of the Scriptures when older copies wore out. Tradition tells us that these scribes were so painstaking in their work that they devised a system to count every word on a scroll to verify that the manuscript they copied was an accurate copy. With this care, they believed the newer copies would actually be more accurate then the tattered and aged older copies.

The scribes then placed the older copies in jars of clay and buried them so they would not be used. Because of this practice, we don't have a huge collection of ancient copies of the Old Testament. In 1947, Bedouin shepherds discovered Old Testament manuscripts in the Qumran caves near the Dead Sea. These manuscripts had been lost for 2,000 years. Over the next decade, many other scrolls were discovered in caves. Every book in the Hebrew Bible, except Esther, was represented in this discovery. Numerous copies of most books were discovered. Thirty copies of Deuteronomy were found. These texts have verified the accuracy and consistency of the copies of the Hebrew Bible. The Great Isaiah Scroll, a copy of the Book of Isaiah, was found in the caves and is nearly word-for-word identical to our standard Hebrew manuscripts. The slight variations that exist are explainable through slight slips of the pen or variations in spelling.

What about the New Testament? Unlike the Old Testament scribes, the people who copied the New Testament did not see the need to bury worn out copies. Thus, we have over 5,600 manuscripts of various portions of the New Testament. The total number of manuscripts is amazing compared to a work like Homer's *Iliad*, one of the most famous ancient books in history of which we have less than 700 copies.

Biblical manuscripts contain rare, minor variants. In most cases, we can discern what is correct from context, parallel passages, and the credibility of other manuscripts. Among these manuscripts there is 99 percent consistency.[6] In no instance does the variant affect the doctrine of Scripture or question core doctrines of the Christian faith.

Variants don't affect the message of the Bible and don't undermine the reliability of the Bible. We know from text messaging and the auto-correct feature on our smart phones that we can still understand 100 percent of the message of a text even when there is a minor variant. In fact, one must make a distinction between the text and its intended message, for one can receive a text with variants and still receive 100 percent of the message.

Conclusion

If we believe Jesus' words as He quoted Deuteronomy 8:3, that no one lives by bread alone "but on every word that comes from the mouth of God" (Matt. 4:4), then we will give the Word a place of prominence in our lives. If we believe Moses when he said the Word of God is our very life, then we will demonstrate our dependence on the Word by reading it with great eagerness and expectation. The apostle Peter believed we should approach the Word the way a newborn baby approaches milk—as the very source of life (1 Pet. 2:2). Thank God for His Word that gives us life and power to accomplish His mission!

Devotions

THE WORD ENDURES FOREVER

1 Peter 1:24-25: "For All flesh is like grass, and all its glory like a flower of the grass. The grass withers, and the flower falls, but the word of the Lord endures forever. And this is the word that was preached as the gospel to you."

What lasts forever? Nothing, it seems. Cars die. We lose shape. iPods get replaced with iPhones. Buildings crumble. No one really disputes it. Our own experience tells us that nothing endures forever. So when Peter says the Word of God lasts forever, it should shock us. We don't even know how long forever is because nothing around us will last that long.

The Word of God shows how frail human life is, how humans are like grass, living short and temporary lives. How foolish it is to think that life is somehow secure, that it is guaranteed that I will even live to an old age. There is nothing certain, nothing secure, and so to receive another year is truly a gift from God. I did not will my life into existence, nor can I will another year of life for myself. It was given to me.

Knowing that life is frail and that I cannot guarantee even one day of life for myself or my loved ones, what is the best usage of my life? Is it to amass as much as possible in as little time as possible? Is it to gain world renown and fame? Money? Power? No, such things don't last forever. The best usage of my life would be to invest in the things that do.

Peter said that what will never perish are those who are living by the enduring Word of God (1 Pet. 1:23), for this is the Word that we hear when we are born again. It is a Word filled with life-giving and life-sustaining power.

Pause and Reflect

1   Do you believe that God's Word lasts forever?

----

2   Do you have some dreams and desires that are not based on God's Word? Consider what 1 John 2:16 says about these desires.

----

3   What are some of your desires that are built on God's Word?

Did God Really Say...?

Genesis 3:1: "Now the serpent was the most cunning of all the wild animals that the LORD God had made. He said to the woman, 'Did God really say, "You can't eat from any tree in the garden"?'"

Words! What are they anyway? Are they just a collection of syllables that come out of our mouths everyday, all day? It is said that the average woman speaks 20,000 words a day; the average man, 7,000. They roll off our tongues most of the time with little to no thought. But aren't our words more than just organized and meaningful sounds that we understand? I think they are.

When we speak, we are an echo of a greater Speaker. We speak because God speaks. He spoke all things into existence. He holds all things together by His Word. He rules the world by His Word. When we deny God's Word, we are denying His rule. In creation, God, in His divine wisdom, made a beautiful garden and put creatures in it. He created a special kind of creature made in His own image to know and love Him. These creatures took their unique gift as image bearers of God and used it to ignore what He said. This changed everything.

You see, to know God means that we live under His good rule and purposes, and to do that, we must listen to and obey Him. So we see that words are at the center of all of reality. We should not be surprised, then, to read how John described the Son of God: "In the beginning was the Word, and the Word was with God, and the Word was God" (John 1:1). When this Word came to our world, the serpent's question "Did God really say...?" was answered. Yes, He really said. And He has spoken again, for the Word took on flesh to dwell among humanity to make the Father known.

Pause and Reflect

1   Does knowing that God really speaks make you want to hear from Him?

2   What does it mean that God speaks for our good?

PURE SPIRITUAL MILK

1 Peter 2:2-3: "Like newborn infants, desire the pure spiritual milk, so that you may grow by it for your salvation since you have tasted that the Lord is good."

Have you ever been around infants getting hungry? It is kind of cute to watch. They begin smacking or licking their lips; opening and closing their mouths; and sucking on hands, fingers, toes, toys, or clothing. If we don't get those early signs, they start squirming around a lot. If that doesn't work, then they start crying and refusing to be soothed by anything except milk.

When we watch hungry babies, it is clear that they have single-minded focus, one desire. Nothing else matters except for the food they need. That is the picture Peter painted to illustrate how we should view the Word of God. But the truth is we are not much like that. Our schedules change and we skip our daily Bible reading. We sit down to read the Scriptures and our minds race through our responsibilities.

What would our lives be like if we approached the Bible the same way infants approach milk? Can we even imagine coming to it hungry and not leaving until we are full? Can we even imagine living with such an awareness of our need for the Word that we read it with single-minded focus? It is hard to imagine it, but that is what we are called to.

Peter said two things after this infant illustration. He said it is by the Word that we grow in our salvation (v. 2b) and that we will come to it with an infant-like dependence if we know that the Lord is good (v. 3). Maybe this is the secret to increasing our appetite for the Scriptures—Remember God's goodness toward us in the gospel, and desire to know more of that goodness as you grow in your salvation.

Pause and Reflect

1   What are you hungry for in your life?

---

2   How does that compare to tasting the goodness of God?

DISCUSSION QUESTIONS

1   Describe something that's been passed down to you through your family
     (a particular item, not a trait). What is your attitude toward it?

- -

2   Do you think the following phrase is helpful or lacking: "God said it;
     I believe it; that settles it"? Why is it important to understand the way God
     gave us His Word?

- -

3   In your own words, how would you explain to someone what it means for
     the Bible to be "God-breathed"? How does the truth of inspiration shape
     the way you approach Scripture?

- -

4   Because God chose not to override the personalities of the Bible's
     authors, how might God use our own personalities and circumstances for
     His purposes?

- -

5   In what ways is it proper to say Scripture is "alive"? How does the life-
     giving nature of Scripture give us hope in the power of Scripture to guide
     our daily lives?

- -

6   Some people consider other documents and texts as "living" in the sense
     that contemporary society should readily adapt and revise them to suit
     current concerns. In what way does inspiration of the Bible contrast with
     this idea of compromising the Scriptures?

- -

7   If you had to come up with a set of characteristics necessary to recognize a
     book of the Bible as "sacred," what would it include? How do you think the
     early Christians came to agreement on which books were inspired?

- -

8   Were you aware of all that went into putting the Bible together? How does
     it help to know the care that went into the establishment of a biblical book
     as sacred?

- -

9   How do each of the functions of God's Word in 2 Timothy 3:16-17 relate to
     our mission as believers?

- -

10   When you look at how the Bible has been preserved over centuries, how
     does this affect the way you value it as God's Word? How might your view
     of Scripture change if it were extremely difficult to obtain a copy?

Chapter 4

By Keith Whitfield

The Bible (Part 2)

Can We Trust the Bible?

VOICES FROM *the Church*

"Even as a mighty cathedral would be unduly darkened and underappreciated if illuminated by only one pinhole window, so too the intricacies and beauty of God's revelation in Jesus the Christ deserve a flood of light from all sides of the building. Our four Gospels all open onto the same inner sanctum and altar, but with different and complementary angles of light." [1]

–Jonathan Pennington

VOICES FROM *Church History*

"If Christianity is false it cannot be saved by theology, if it is true it cannot be destroyed by science." [2]

–E. Y. Mullins (1860-1928)

In recent years, publishers have dealt with the problem of "fake memoirs." While literary forgery is nothing new, this particular form draws a great deal of attention. People present details from their lives that simply are not true. Readers believe the stories and sometimes are personally affected by them. Then, when the lies are revealed, there is a public outcry.

One of the most famous examples was a story told by Herman Rosenblat, a Holocaust survivor. He developed a love story about a little girl throwing apples to him over the fence of his concentration camp every day for a few months. Years later, he went on a blind date and discovered the woman was the same little girl. He proposed to her on the spot, and they were married.

Rosenblat's story earned him an invitation to "The Oprah Winfrey Show." Later, he sought to publish his memoir. Plans for a movie were in the works. Before the memoir was released, however, it became clear that although he had met his wife on a blind date, many other details of the story were false—no little girl; no apples. Rosenblat had developed a love story that tugged at the heartstrings of America. Unfortunately, it wasn't real.

Some today question the integrity of the Bible's historical accounts. They see the Gospels as exaggerated fables based on a true person (in this case, Jesus) who never would have sanctioned the authors' portrayals. Or perhaps they see apparent contradictions in the Gospels and question the truthfulness of the authors. If we are to embrace a biblical worldview, it's important that we answer the question "Can we trust the Bible?"

In this chapter, we will examine three common questions about the Bible's truthfulness. First, we will consider the claim that there are contradictions between the biblical accounts. Then, we will examine the claim that historical and scientific research have proven the Bible untrue. Finally, we will look at several reasons why we can and should trust the Bible as truth without any mixture of error.

Doesn't the Bible contradict itself? (Matt. 1:1-17; Luke 3:23-38)

As Christians, we believe the Bible is the inspired Word of God. We believe the Old and New Testament authors wrote under the direction of the Holy Spirit (2 Sam. 23:2; Matt. 22:43). The apostle Paul declared, "All Scripture is inspired by God" (2 Tim. 3:16). Jesus Himself described the Scripture as the very word that comes from the mouth of God (Matt. 4:4).

While the Bible attests to being God's Word, not everyone believes it is truly from the mouth of God and true in all it teaches. People claim there are contradictions and errors in the Bible. Here are a few common objections:

- *That just can't happen.* This objection looks at miraculous events recorded in Scripture and concludes that because these types of things don't happen around us every day, these events could never happen according to the natural world order. This reasoning leads people to conclude that what the Bible says about miracles must be false.
- *That's not the way the world works.* This objection criticizes the biblical descriptions of natural phenomena, such as the sun rising (Ps. 19:6), and concludes the Bible is untrue in its descriptions of this sort. After all, we all know the sun does not really rise; the earth moves around the sun.
- *That contradicts what someone else says over here.* This objection analyzes and points out the conflict between two statements or descriptions. It could be two biblical statements that seem to contradict each other or a biblical statement held up against a contradictory statement from a historical source.

Let's start with the objection about contradictions in the Bible. At first glance, sections in the Bible may appear to contradict each other. A case in point are the birth narratives of Jesus. Both Matthew 1:1-17 and Luke 3:23-38 are genealogies of Jesus and trace the lineage of Jesus through history.

Matthew's account traces the line of descent from Abraham to Jesus in 42 generations, while Luke's account begins the ancestry with Jesus and works backward all the way to Adam in 76 generations. Why are there differences? To understand this issue, it's important to remember the purpose in the mind of each author.

Matthew's genealogy is concise. It is organized in three groups of 14, connecting the line to three time periods. The first group lists the patriarchs, the second names the kings, and the third contains ordinary citizens. The intent was not to give a strict record but rather to present the historical progression. It begins by highlighting the family origin, then the rise to power through David's throne, and eventually the decline from royalty to the humble birth of the Messiah. By relating Jesus to David and Abraham, Matthew's genealogy shows the relationship of Jesus to all Jews—He is their Messiah. This coincides with the overarching theme and purpose of the Book of Matthew—to prove that Jesus is, in fact, the long-awaited Messiah.

Luke's account, however, begins in a unique way for a genealogy. It begins with Jesus and moves backward through history to Adam. Some suggest that Luke's purpose in ordering the genealogy this way is to emphasize the grand significance of Jesus. Perhaps another purpose in Luke's order is to highlight that the Messiah is a fully human Savior. His genealogy of Jesus is traced all the way back to Adam, demonstrating the relationship of Jesus to all of mankind.

While the two genealogies are nearly identical from Abraham to David, they are entirely different from David to Jesus. After David, only three names appear on both lists. Even more significant is that the grandfather and father for Joseph are different in the two accounts.

Skeptics usually attribute the differences between these two genealogies to biblical errors. But there are additional ideas on how to resolve the apparent contradictions.

• *Luke supplies Jesus' human lineage through Joseph, while Matthew gives his legal lineage by which He is the legitimate successor to the throne.* This explanation points us to the custom of the kinsman redeemer—if a man died without bearing a son, then his brother would marry his widow and their firstborn son would carry on the name of the deceased husband. This would make Matthan's son, Jacob, Joseph's legal father and Matthat's son, Heli, Joseph's biological father. Matthew's account would trace Jesus' legal lineage, and Luke's record would follow Jesus' biological lineage.

• *Luke presents Mary's genealogy, while Matthew relates Joseph's genealogy.* This possible explanation would account for the different names for the grandfather and father of Joseph.

These are two of the more popular explanations for the apparent contradictions between Matthew's and Luke's genealogies, yet even these are not without their difficulties. Certainty of explanation may be beyond us, but certainty of the message is clear—Jesus is the true heir to the throne of David, no matter how you trace His lineage. And it should be noted that the early Christians overwhelmingly accepted the divine authority of these two Gospels, meaning the perceived contradiction is just that—perceived.

- -

Recommendations for Dealing with Difficult Texts in the Bible

1. Be sure that you are interacting with real texts, not uninformed accusations from others.
2. Approach the text in trust, not as a skeptic.
3. Pray about the difficult text in question.
4. Don't demand that ancient writers conform to your expected standards (demanding perfectly parallel, verbatim quotations, for example).
5. Seek counsel when dealing with difficult texts.
6. Be willing to set aside a text for further consideration rather than force harmonization. [3]

Hasn't the Bible been proven untrue? (Luke 2:1-3)

We've looked briefly at the charge that the Bible contradicts itself. What about apparent contradictions in the matter of science? Or history? Biblical authority is challenged today from every conceivable perspective, from scientific, to religious, to historical objections.

But let's go back to the Christmas account for another look at another common objection. In Luke 2:1-3, Luke tells us the historical circumstances surrounding Joseph and Mary's trip to Bethlehem.

> 1 *In those days a decree went out from Caesar Augustus that the whole empire should be registered.* 2 *This first registration took place while Quirinius was governing Syria.* 3 *So everyone went to be registered, each to his own town.*

This account raises a significant historical problem. Luke connects the circumstances surrounding Jesus' birth to the census of Quirinius. Some scholars find multiple problems with this account:

1. There is no historical evidence that Quirinius ordered a census during the time of Jesus' birth. According to Josephus, he ordered one in A.D. 6, and it was considered innovative.
2. There is no record of an empire-wide census while Augustus was emperor.
3. A Roman census would not have required Joseph to return to Bethlehem.
4. The well-known records of the Roman governors do not list Quirinius as governor at the time of Jesus' birth.
5. Thus, there would have been no census in Palestine during the time of Herod the Great.

Scholars may find Luke's account to be historically implausible, but that's usually because they're discounting Luke's testimony from the start, as if they assume Luke to be less reliable than other historical sources.

Furthermore, there are a number of explanations that back up Luke's account. First, the possibility of the census occurring at this time (and Joseph needing to travel to Bethlehem) is supported by the fact that Augustus issued three censuses during the time of Jesus' birth, and the Romans would allow people to follow their own customs when it came to registering.

What's more, there are numerous solutions to the reference to Quirinius. One of the strongest is that there is evidence that Quirinius was serving as governor of Syria in 6-4 B.C. and also in A.D. 6-9. While we may not be certain of the exact dates, we can be sure the proposed solutions are as credible, if not more so, than the objections on this point.

What we discover from these two accounts surrounding Jesus' incarnation is that there are multiple perspectives by which we can approach a text. How we approach the Bible affects what we see and how we understand what the text is saying.

No one should ignore the questions these texts raise. But we must be careful not to examine the questions from a perspective that limits us from seeing possible ways to resolve the issues. What we've discovered time and again with these objections is that these criticisms often arise from a set of commitments, a set of preconceived notions about the world, that are in conflict with the biblical view of the world.

Another common objection is the one we mentioned earlier—that science has disproved the Bible and the miracles described there. But this objection begins with the unproven assumption that God does not exist or that miracles simply cannot occur. In other words, the starting point is one that declares the Bible to be false in its testimony regarding the existence and power of God.

But what if we start with the Bible? There we see the world was designed with a purpose and was created by an all-powerful, personal God. God's personal nature makes a difference in how we understand our world. A personal God acts with purpose. He is loving. He provides. He makes Himself known to His creation. He is all-powerful. Thus, He can do whatever He wants to do, and nothing stops Him.

These are big truths that have implications in how we see the miracle stories of the Bible. First off, miraculous works are no challenge at all to an all-powerful, personal God.

Second, accurately describing the way the world works is no challenge to the Creator of all things. We recognize that in some cases the Bible may be using language the way we often use language—figuratively. When we say we watched the sunrise at the beach, no one accuses us of lying, of putting forth a scientific study that claims the sun rises above the eastern horizon. Expressing a truth from our human vantage point is not error.

Finally, if the Bible comes from a personal, all-powerful God, then possible contradictions within the biblical stories or with historical documents cannot easily be dismissed as errors. Instead, we ought to see how the Bible coheres and, when in doubt, give the Bible the benefit of the doubt.

These responses do not answer all the objections that people raise against the Bible, but what they do show is that one's approach to the Scriptures (whether they are suspicious or humble) has a great deal to do with their view of God and His relationship to the world.

It's good to remember that providing evidence for the truthfulness of Scripture will probably not convince a skeptic. Most of the time, the one who doubts the biblical account also doubts the fundamental claim of Scripture— that there is a personal, all-powerful God at work in the world.

Jesus gave us an example of how our view of God affects our approach to His Word. In John 17, He prayed to His Father to protect His people with His Word. The way the Word protects them is by sanctifying them, freeing them from "the lust of the flesh, the lust of the eyes and the pride in one's lifestyle" (1 John 2:16). Jesus prayed this way because He knew the One who gave the Word, and He knew that the power of the Word would protect God's people.

Why should I trust the Bible?

Why trust the Bible? Throughout the Scriptures, the biblical authors recognized that their writing was under the direction of the Holy Spirit (2 Sam. 23:2; Matt. 22:43; 2 Pet. 1:21). But the biggest reason we as Christians trust the Bible is *because Jesus Himself did*.

Because Scripture is the Word of God, Jesus honored and cherished it. He said it was imperishable (Matt. 5:17-18). He claimed it would not fail in its purpose and could not be broken (John 10:35). He held up its supremacy over human tradition (Matt. 15:3,6). And He considered the Bible to be historically reliable (Matt. 12:40; 24:37-38).

The Bible is a historical book. The events it describes took place in history. The Bible does not contain theological truths unrelated to history. History matters! It is for this reason Paul argued that if Christ's bodily resurrection did not happen in history, then our faith is futile (1 Cor. 15:17).

Just as the resurrection has never been disproved, neither has the Bible been disproved. We have many reasons to believe the Bible is what it claims to be— the very Word of God. Here are three: *the Bible's unity, its central message, and its transforming power*.

First, we trust the Bible because of its unity. The biblical story is one grand story from Genesis to Revelation. This story unfolds through multiple plots and subplots. In the midst of all the themes, all the people, and all the stories, there is one central theme through the Scriptures—the promise and fulfillment of a messianic King who is establishing an eternal kingdom for God. This grand story points to one Person, Jesus Christ (Luke 24:27). In the Old Testament, Christ is promised to the people of God. In the New Testament, He arrives (Matt. 5:17-18). The detailed nature of the prophecies fulfilled in Jesus is one of the clearest signs that the Bible is no ordinary book.

Next, related to the unity of Scripture is the central message of Scripture for the people of God. From the fall of Adam and Eve in the garden to the coming of Jesus at the end, the Bible teaches one clear central message. All humanity has sinned and is in need of a Savior (Gen. 6:5; Rom. 3:23), and salvation through Christ is the only solution (Mark 10:45; Luke 19:10).

Finally, we should trust the Scripture because of its transforming power (John 20:31; Heb. 4:12). The story of the Ethiopian eunuch in Acts 8 is only one example of how the proclamation of Scripture changes the heart and brings new life. Many of us know this from our own personal experience and the experiences of those around us. The Bible tells a story that through the supernatural work of the Holy Spirit, God can change a heart of stone into a heart that loves and worships our Creator.

Conclusion

Trusting the truthfulness of the Scripture is first a matter of trusting that God is there and He is not silent, as Francis Schaeffer liked to say. These two beliefs not only help us explain how God speaks, but they also guide us as we seek to understand and engage the questions that come up in reading the Bible. We may stumble over certain things we read, but we humbly seek to understand what is being said because we believe it comes from God Himself and for the empowerment of our mission.

- -

VOICES FROM *the Church*

"Trusting testimony is not an irrational act of faith that leaves critical rationality aside; it is, on the contrary, the rationally appropriate way of responding to authentic testimony. Gospels understood as testimony are the entirely appropriate means of access to the historical reality of Jesus."[4]
–Richard Bauckham

Devotions

APPROACHING THE BIBLE

What is the Bible? Does it matter what you think about it? Is it inspired or man-made, without error or faulty, myth or history? How you answer these questions matters.

The Bible itself claims to be the very words of God and not simply a book of stories and morals truths. His Word is not given to satisfy your curiosity about God. His Word is given that we might be satisfied in Him, know Him, and love Him.

God breathed out His Word so that we should inhale it. In a real sense, that is how we remain connected to the vital, life-transforming life of God. We must take in God's Word in order to live spiritually and to grow in our love and obedience to God.

How do you approach reading the Scriptures? As your Christian duty? Overwhelmed with the thought of where to start? Out of curiosity, to learn more facts about the Bible?

Paul told us what the purpose of Scripture is and how to approach it in Romans 15:4. He said, "For whatever was written in the past was written for our instruction, so that we may have hope through endurance and through the encouragement from the Scriptures." The picture here is of two things coming together, creating a spark that makes a fire. The instruction we get from Scripture rubs up against our lives in the midst of circumstances, challenges, and temptations. "Striking" our circumstances with the instruction of Scripture produces burning hope and encouragement. Paul's use of the word "through" points to an ongoing interaction between the Word and our lives.

Pause and Reflect

1   What are your expectations from your Bible reading?

---

2   What is one passage that you've read recently that you can use to seek hope through endurance?

---

3   Do you desire the Bible like medicine, like food, like air? Is it producing in you faith-filled hope and encouragement?

Delight in the Word

The Book of Psalms begins by giving us a picture of a glorious way of life. It begins: "How happy is the man who does not follow the advice of the wicked or take the path of sinners or join a group of mockers! Instead, his delight is in the LORD's instruction, and he meditates on it day and night" (Ps. 1:1-2). The picture is of a person described as living in happiness, or blessedness.

How does that sound to you? Do you want to be blessed? Do you want to be steadfast in your faith regardless of your circumstances? Do you want to bear spiritual fruit in your life? Do you want to prosper in your love and service toward others? The psalmist told us there is a way!

What is the pathway to this incredible flourishing of life? Delight in the Word of God and meditate on it day and night! Those who are blessed give themselves to delighting in the Word of God and meditating on it day and night. Then the psalmist illustrated this life as a tree planted where its roots get nutrients and its limbs produce fruit (v. 3). Over the well-being of this person the Lord watches (v. 6).

These verses are not merely good advice. These are promises. The one who gives himself to the Word will be blessed, will produce fruit, and will be protected by God. Do you delight in the Word? If not, pray this: "Turn my eyes from looking at what is worthless; give me life in Your ways. Confirm what you said to Your servant, for it produces reverence for You" (Ps. 119:37-38)

Pause and Reflect

1   Can you insert your name in this sentence? How happy is _____!

----

2   Do you trust the promises of Psalm 1?

----

3   Pray Psalm 119:37-38.

Passing On the Word

The Old Testament introduces us to the God who speaks. He had Moses gather the redeemed Israelites before Him so that He could speak to them and so they would hear His voice. "Assemble the people before Me, and I will let them hear My words, so that they may learn to fear Me all the days they live on the earth and may instruct their children" (Deut. 4:10).

Can you imagine being there? Six hundred thousand men with many more women and children assembled around Mount Sinai—"blazing with fire into the heavens and enveloped in a dense, black cloud" (Deut. 4:11). That would have been quite a sight!

The words God spoke were the path of life for Israel. They were the way to know their Redeemer and follow His ways. These words were so vital to the people of Israel that they were not meant to die or fade away. The message was meant to be passed on from generation to generation. The God who speaks has a Word that lasts forever.

There is a real sense that all the people of God for every age were represented in that assembly around the mountain. That word was passed down for us. And we are to pass it along as well.

Parents have an important role to play in this. When we teach our children from the Bible, it is more than passing along just another tradition. It is more than teaching a set of rules or a moral code. We are instructing them in the message of the God of the universe who created the world by His word. When we instruct our children, we are joining God in His mission

Pause and Reflect

1   How does it make you feel to know that the word God spoke to Israel around Mount Sinai was meant for you too?

----

2   How are you called to pass along God's Word to the next generation?

DISCUSSION QUESTIONS

1   Do you enjoy reading memoirs? In what ways does knowing a story is true enhance your reading? What are the signs a person's testimony is true? Exaggerated or imagined?

2   What is the connection between a person's trustworthy character and the validity of their testimony?

3   What objections or apparent contradictions have you seen cause doubts in the trustworthiness of the Bible?

4   What are the biggest differences between the genealogies of Jesus in Matthew and Luke? What other differences between accounts have you found in the Bible?

5   How does understanding the author's purpose help us make sense of apparent differences between biblical accounts?

6   What are some charges made against Christianity that often come around Christmas and Easter?

7   Let's say you're having a conversation with a friend who has seen a documentary questioning the biblical account of Christ's birth. How would you respond? What resources would you turn to in order to answer the charge?

8   Have you ever been tempted to question the authority and truthfulness of the Scriptures? What was your view of God during that time? How does your view of who God is affect the way you approach the Scriptures?

9   How does Jesus' perspective on the Scripture's reliability help us trust the Bible in places we don't understand?

10 In what ways does the transforming power of the Scripture lead us to greater missionary fervor? Why is it important for Christians to be equipped to deal with difficult passages as we share the gospel?

Chapter 5

By Afshin Ziafat

One Among Many?

Christianity Is Unique Among the Religion

Voices from *Church History*

"If [Jesus] is not what He claims, there is nothing in religion; it is pure fiction. If, however, Jesus Christ is not a humbug, and not a dreamer, but what He claims to be, then Christianity is the grandest fact that ever was introduced to any man."[1]
–Oswald Chambers (1874-1917)

Voices from *the Church*

"Why does Jesus say He's the only way?…[Because] no one else is coming for you. There is no other God who loves you and passionately pursues you and longs to forgive you of your sin and heal you from your brokenness."[2]
–Erwin McManus

The Self-Realization Lake Shrine in California is advertised as a spiritual sanctuary where one can retreat to hear the voice of God. In the midst of its beautiful gardens, paths, and natural spring-fed lake is an area called the Court of Religions, created in honor of the five principal world religions.

In this court you find five markers with the names and symbols of these religions: Christianity, Judaism, Islam, Hinduism, and Buddhism. All five markers are identical with the exception of the name and symbol, illustrating one of the leading thoughts in our world today. Many people view all the world's religions as different paths leading to the same place and the same person—God. The path one takes is a matter of personal preference, but any of them will "work" and lead you to eternity with God as long as you sincerely pursue the path.

Standing against the idea that all religions lead to God are the words of Jesus Christ. In John 14:6, Jesus made a claim to be the exclusive path to God, saying, "I am the way, the truth, and the life. No one comes to the Father except through Me." In this chapter, we will examine this assertion of Jesus Christ and see how Christ's person, His teaching, and His resurrection make Christianity unique among all the world religions. Christ's uniqueness is good news for a lost world.

Jesus is unique because of who He is (the Way).

What makes something unique? People love to jump on the bandwagon of the latest fad or fashion. Something "original" pops up, and we are drawn to it. Soon, with everyone wearing the same style of clothes or listening to the same "fresh" song, the uniqueness wears off. It becomes old hat. What was once "unique" starts to look "old."

Many people view Christianity this way. It's a "classic" religious option with a timeless feel to it, but it's certainly not new, exciting, and fresh. Hinduism may seem more exotic, or Buddhism more acceptable, or Islam more rigorous. Or maybe the best approach is to disregard religious identity altogether and become one of "the nones"—the growing number of people in society who check "none of the above" about their religious affiliation.

It makes sense to move from one religion to another if *uniqueness* means novel or exciting. But it doesn't make sense if we are using the term *unique* in its biblical sense—one-of-a-kind, superior, or only. And that's just the kind of uniqueness Jesus claimed for Himself. Not the faddish pursuit of novelty for its own sake but the settled confidence on display in who He is and what He taught.

Before His arrest, Jesus spent the last hours of His earthly ministry with His disciples. At the last supper, He told them about His impending departure. They did not understand that He was referring to His death on the cross and His subsequent resurrection. Jesus comforted them with the truth that what He would accomplish would be a great benefit to them.

The apostle John recorded a crucial part of this conversation in John 14:1-11:

1 *"Your heart must not be troubled. Believe in God; believe also in Me.* 2 *In My Father's house are many dwelling places; if not, I would have told you. I am going away to prepare a place for you.* 3 *If I go away and prepare a place for you, I will come back and receive you to Myself, so that where I am you may be also.* 4 *You know the way to where I am going."*

5 *"Lord," Thomas said, "we don't know where You're going. How can we know the way?"*

6 *Jesus told him, "I am the way, the truth, and the life. No one comes to the Father except through Me.* 7 *If you know Me, you will also know My Father. From now on you do know Him and have seen Him."*

8 *"Lord," said Philip, "show us the Father, and that's enough for us."*

9 *Jesus said to him, "Have I been among you all this time without your knowing Me, Philip? The one who has seen Me has seen the Father. How can you say, 'Show us the Father'?* 10 *Don't you believe that I am in the Father and the Father is in Me? The words I speak to you I do not speak on My own. The Father who lives in Me does His works.* 11 *Believe Me that I am in the Father and the Father is in Me. Otherwise, believe because of the works themselves.*

In this passage we see that Jesus was leaving His disciples in order to prepare a place for them to remain with Him forever. When Jesus told them they knew the way, the disciples responded with confusion. Thomas said, "We don't know where You are going. How can we know the way?"

Thomas' point was simple enough: If the disciples didn't know the destination, then how could they know the path? They thought if they knew "where" Jesus was going, then they could figure out how to follow Him there. They missed the crucial fact that Jesus Himself was both the destination and the path. Jesus was not saying, "My way will be your way." He was saying, "Your way is ME!"

This misinterpretation of Jesus' statement sheds light on the tendency of human beings to erroneously think we are self-sufficient. We think "the way" lies in ourselves. "I did it my way," sang Frank Sinatra, and in one way or another, this has been the song of the human heart since the beginning of human history. (In fact, the Bible teaches that this thirst for independence is what initially got us in trouble!)

The prophet Isaiah reminded us of our past when he wrote, "We all went astray like sheep; we all have turned to our own way" (Isa. 53:6). God told the first humans that if they ate from the tree, then they would die. By turning to their own way, Adam and Eve followed the way that led humankind to death. "There is a way that seems right to man, but its end is the way to death" (Prov. 14:12).

In contrast to going our own way, Jesus claims to be the way. He is the path and destination. The path to God is not a list of actions. It is a Person.

Likewise, the ultimate reward is not heaven but Jesus—the One whose presence makes heaven what it is. If Jesus is the prize of eternal life in heaven, then He must be the pursuit of our temporal lives on earth.

Most religions of the world understand that something has gone wrong in the world and that we need some sort of salvation. What sets Christianity apart from the world's religions is the solution to the problem of sin. Jesus not only points to the solution, He is the solution.

Other religions of the world offer a way to return to God's favor by religiosity, good works, or self-effort. The problem with this approach is that the strategy to get us out of our sin problem is the same strategy that caused us to get into our sin problem in the first place—going our own way! Self-effort can never get us back into a right standing with God.

As an example, the religion of Islam presents a works-based path to God. When I was a Muslim, I was taught that all my deeds in life would be accounted for and written down by angels. Furthermore, I was warned that on the Day of Judgment, my deeds would be weighed upon scales. God would approve me if my scales were proven to be heavy in good deeds.

Like most religions, this teaching puts much of the focus on human effort. But when I became a Christian, I saw the stark contrast between grace and works. Whereas most religions are essentially man's attempt to make a way back to God, only in Christianity can one find the truth that God took the initiative and made His way to man. Jesus is the way because He is the only One who could die in our place and be raised again, removing our sin and death to reconcile us to God.

If Jesus is the way to God, how are we to respond? Since Jesus has already made the way through His death and resurrection, it makes no sense for us to try to make it to God through our own self-effort. That would be as fruitless as boarding an airplane, taking your seat, buckling your seatbelt, and then flapping your arms as if that would help you get to your destination. No, all you need to do is get on the plane.

Similarly, our response to Christ's words is to be united with Him in faith. "For if we have been joined with Him in the likeness of His death, we will certainly also be in the likeness of His resurrection" (Rom. 6:5).

Jesus is unique because of what He says (the Truth).

Since Christ's grand statement in John 14:6 was precipitated by a discussion about the "way," we should view His claims to be the "truth" and the "life" as being supports for Jesus being the "way." Because Jesus is the "truth," He alone is the "way" for humans to be reconciled to God.

6 *Jesus told him, "I am the way, the truth, and the life. No one comes to the Father except through Me.*

Jesus is unique because of what He says, primarily about Himself. He doesn't just claim to speak the truth. He claims to be the truth.

What does this statement mean? Jesus is the truth because He embodies the supreme revelation of God. He is God's revelation of Himself to us. The Gospel of John portrays Christ as being God's gracious self-disclosure to the world:

- **John 1:14:** *"The Word became flesh and took up residence among us. We observed His glory, the glory as the One and Only Son from the Father, full of grace and truth."* Jesus is the Word that took on flesh and dwelt among us so that we may see the glory of God.
- **John 1:18:** *"No one has ever seen God. The One and Only Son—the One who is at the Father's side—He has revealed Him."* Jesus is the only One who is at the Father's side, and He has made God known to us.
- **John 10:25,30:** *"'I did tell you and you don't believe,' Jesus answered them. 'The works that I do in My Father's name testify about Me...The Father and I are one.'"* Jesus doesn't just represent God. He says He is one with the Father and that His works testify that He exclusively and completely does what the Father says and does.
- **John 14:9-11:** *"Jesus said to him, 'Have I been among you all this time without your knowing Me, Philip? The one who has seen Me has seen the Father. How can you say, "Show us the Father"? Don't you believe that I am in the Father and the Father is in Me? The words I speak to you I do not speak on My own. The Father who lives in Me does His works. Believe Me that I am in the Father and the Father is in Me. Otherwise, believe because of the works themselves.'"* To reject Jesus is to reject God Himself. But to see, hear, and believe Jesus is to see, hear, and believe God.

The Book of Hebrews describes the uniqueness of Jesus in a similar manner, saying God has spoken in the past through prophets but in these last days by His Son (Heb. 1:1-2). It is important for us to see Jesus as more than a prophet or religious leader who speaks the truths of God. He Himself is the truth that reveals God to us.

The uniqueness of Christianity is Jesus. He alone shows us who God is. Notice again the conversation He had with Philip (vv. 9-11). Jesus claimed to be the way to God because of who He was in relation to God.

If we are to take Jesus at His word, we must reject the popular notion of the day that Jesus is just one of many valid truths about God. It is precisely because Jesus is the sole truth of God that He says "no one comes to the Father except through Me" (John 14:6).

We're tempted to shy away from the exclusive claim of Christ in this passage. We worry such a narrow assertion will not be appealing in our modern world. But ironically, throughout Christian history, it's the uniqueness and exclusivity of Jesus Christ that has given Christianity its lasting relevance!

The early Christians didn't hide their beliefs: "There is salvation in no one else, for there is no other name under heaven given to people, and we must be saved by it" (Acts 4:12). Jesus Himself instructed His followers to enter by the narrow gate for "the gate is wide and the road is broad that leads to destruction, and there are many who go through it" (Matt. 7:13).

To take away the exclusive part of the truth of Christ is to take away the entire truth of Christ. If you try to make Jesus just "one of many," you lose Jesus the "One and Only."

Two Kinds of Tolerance

The traditional definition of *tolerance* accepts the existence of other viewpoints and recognizes that other people have the right to hold different beliefs or practices. The newer understanding of *tolerance* means one accepts the other viewpoints as true or valid. D. A. Carson writes: "To accept that a different or opposing position exists and deserves the right to exist is one thing; to accept the position itself means that one is no longer opposing it."[3]

People in our society often confuse religious tolerance with relativism. Rightly understood, tolerance is accepting that people should be able to coexist with different religious beliefs. Wrongly understood, tolerance means all religious beliefs are equal—"What's true for you may be true for you but not for me." Jesus shatters this notion. He is not the truth for me or for you only. He is the truth for everybody.

Jesus is unique because of what He does (the Life).

Not only does Jesus claim to be the way and the truth, He also claims to be the life. He is the life, and He demonstrates this claim by dying on the cross for our sins and rising again to new life. Jesus is unique because He is the only Savior who has died and risen again.

6 *Jesus told him, "I am the way, the truth, and the life. No one comes to the Father except through Me.*

Jesus' claim to be the life points us to His unique relationship with God. The Bible portrays God as the Giver and Sustainer of life. As stated earlier, because of our sin, we are separated from God and therefore separated from the source of life. That's why we grow old and die. Romans 6:23 tells us that the wages of sin is death.

We need deliverance from death. We need spiritual and physical life. The concept of resurrection is a distinctive belief that sets us apart from other religions. We need our spiritually dead hearts to be made alive. We need our physically dead bodies to be resurrected. Through His death and resurrection, Jesus does what is necessary for our regeneration and resurrection.

Jesus did not come to make us more well-behaved people so God could tolerate us and accept us. Jesus came to make us alive when we were dead.

No other religion portrays the state of humankind quite as starkly as Christianity. We are dead in our sins (Eph. 2:1). Neither does any other religious figure claim to have the power to bring the dead back to life.

Christ is unique in what He does: He comes back to life and He grants life. How does He accomplish this? By removing the curse of sin by becoming a curse for us (Gal. 3:13). Through His death and resurrection, we see Jesus make good on His claim to be the life. His sacrifice was sufficient in the eyes of God to remove our sin, and His sacrifice removed the consequence of sin, which is death (Rom. 6:23).

Jesus' resurrection also ensures the future resurrection of those who belong to him by faith. Paul writes: "For since death came through a man, the resurrection of the dead also comes through a man. For as in Adam all die, so also in Christ all will be made alive. But each in his own order: Christ, the firstfruits; afterward, at His coming, those who belong to Christ" (1 Cor. 15:21-23).

The response of the Christian to Jesus' unbending claims about Himself is not to soften His words but to proclaim as His ambassadors the salvation that comes through Him alone. That's why we are called to declare the truth that eternal life is available to anyone who will repent of their sin and put their trust in Christ.

Jesus proclaimed: "I am the resurrection and the life. The one who believes in Me, even if he dies, will live. Everyone who lives and believes in Me will never die—ever" (John 11:25-26). We see in this text that Jesus refers to a death that everyone experiences and a death that some will not experience because of faith in him. The first death is a physical death that all mankind experiences. The second death is an eternal spiritual death and separation from God—and death is what Jesus came to save us from.

Those who belong to Christ immediately pass over into eternal life and in the future will not come under the judgment that leads to eternal death. "I assure you: Anyone who hears My word and believes Him who sent Me has eternal life and will not come under judgment but has passed from death to life" (John 5:24). Even more, we are assured a final resurrection so that even physical death will one day be overcome and reversed.

The religions of this world may contain teaching that can make you a well-behaved person on the outside. But only Jesus has the power to bring us from death to life (John 10:10).

Conclusion

Most world religions understand and teach that man has been marred by sin and is separated from God. They all claim to have a path back toward a right standing with God.

• In Islam, one can submit to the Five Pillars in hopes that the balance of good works will earn approval of the person before God.

• In Hinduism, karma stresses the need for good living in order to be reincarnated to a better status until ultimately you are one with the impersonal God.

• Judaism emphasizes that those who are obedient to the law will live forever with God.

• In our postmodern world, the leading belief is that truth is relative and many roads lead to God.

But the uniqueness of Christianity can be seen in the person and work of Jesus Christ. We see that Jesus is unique in who He claims to be as the way. Jesus made a way for mankind when no way was possible for us to travel back to God on our own.

Jesus is unique in what He says as He claims to be the truth. Jesus is the ultimate expression of God, and without knowing Christ, man cannot know God.

Jesus is unique because of what He does. He claims to be the life. And He alone has defeated death through His resurrection. He alone can give life to mankind now and forever. Jesus is the way, the truth, and the life.

Devotions

JESUS IS THE ONE AND ONLY

Acts 4:12: "There is salvation in no one else, for there is no other name under heaven given to people, and we must be saved by it."

Clearly the early church in the Book of Acts believed in an exclusive gospel that portrayed Christ alone as being the means to salvation for mankind. Today, many reject this notion as being arrogant bigotry. Our society lifts up tolerance as the supreme virtue, and by tolerance they mean acceptance of all viewpoints. Truth is said to be relative and any opinion is valid. Furthermore, no religion or worldview can corner the market on truth.

The story of a group of blind men encountering an elephant for the first time supports this view. Each blind man felt the elephant and described it in a unique way. One blind man, who touched the trunk, described the elephant as a snake. Another who touched the leg of the elephant described it as a tree trunk. A third blind man who touched the side of the elephant said the elephant was large and flat. Each blind man could touch only a part of the elephant but couldn't visualize the whole thing. Many view religions this way—they can have part of the truth, but they can't claim to know one comprehensive truth about God.

Many scholars have pointed out that this illustration backfires. Why? Because the story is told from the point of view of someone who is not blind and obviously can see the whole elephant. In other words, the one claiming it's impossible to see the whole truth is saying he can see the whole truth!

In contrast to the elephant illustration, Jesus affirmed His uniqueness and called us to follow the narrow way

Pause and Reflect

1   Why do you think it is hard for people to affirm the idea of absolute truth?

- -

2   What makes Jesus unique and the only One in whom salvation is found?

Jesus Is the Truth

John 8:31-32: "So Jesus said to the Jews who had believed Him, 'If you continue in My word, you really are My disciples. You will know the truth, and the truth will set you free.'"

The religions of the world are replete with prophets who claim to speak on behalf of God. These prophets are said to speak truths that God wants to convey to mankind. However, Jesus claims something else about Himself. He claims to be *the* truth of God. Jesus doesn't just tell us truths about God; He is the ultimate expression of God.

The Gospel of John continually shows us that Jesus reveals God to mankind (John 1:18). Many ask the question "What is God like?" Scripture says the answer is Jesus. Jesus does the works of God and speaks the very words of God (8:28-29). To see and know Jesus is to see and know God. Just as Jesus taught His disciples, the path to knowing Jesus is abiding in His word. If we remain in His word, then we will be true disciples who know the truth about what God is like.

The truth is not a set of rules but Jesus Himself. He is the way, the truth, and the life of God (14:6). Jesus told the Jews who were seeking to kill Him that His word didn't abide in them. He told them that they searched the Scriptures thinking they had life in them, but the Scriptures point to Jesus (5:38-40).

As followers of Christ, we must remember that we come to the Bible not just to learn truths about God. We come to the Bible to meet with Jesus and to know the truth of God. This relationship with Christ (and not just moral truths) is what sets us free from the sins that enslave us.

Pause and Reflect

1   How does your view of Christ change as you consider Him to be the ultimate truth of God?

2   How can you focus your daily life on abiding in His Word?

Jesus Is the Way

Proverbs 3:5-6: "Trust in the LORD with all your heart, and do not rely on your own understanding; think about Him in all your ways, and He will guide you on the right paths."

Most religions of the world teach that mankind has been marred by sin and needs to find a way back to God. The majority of these religions will say that man must work his own way to God through religious activity. Christianity is unique in its insistence that God alone could and has made a way for mankind. In Christ, God has made a way to man, and through Christ's sufficient sacrifice on the cross, God has prepared a way for man.

Therefore, trusting and leaning on Christ alone is the way for all mankind. We receive this salvation by faith—leaning on His finished work and not on our own strength. Similarly, in everyday life, we are called to trust God and not try to control our own lives. When we try to put our hands into God's plan instead of trusting Him, it usually ends up hurting us.

The story of David taking the ark of the covenant into the city of Jerusalem illustrates this for us (1 Chron. 13). There was a prescribed way for David to transport the ark—only the Levites were to carry it with the use of acacia poles on either side. However, David went his own way and wheeled the ark in a cart. As the ark began to fall, a man named Uzzah touched the ark and God struck him dead. David later went back and followed God's way, and it led to rejoicing. Our own way ends in death; God's way leads to life.

Pause and Reflect

1   Why is Jesus' work through His death and resurrection the only way for mankind to be saved?

- -

2   In what areas of your life do you need to trust God and not lean on your own strength or understanding?

Discussion Questions

1 How might you respond to someone who says all religions are equally valid and teach the same thing? In what ways does this mind-set detract from the uniqueness of Jesus?

----

2 Some say that believing Christianity is true leads to hostility toward non-Christians. How does the gospel inform how we treat people of other faiths?

----

3 Buddhism has the Eightfold Path. Islam has the Five Pillars. Other religions are based on teachers who show the way to God. What is the significance of Jesus claiming not only to show the way but to be the way?

----

4 What are some examples of human beings going their own way in attitude and action? How can our trust in Jesus as the way be reflected in our behavior?

----

5 What are the consequences of disbelieving Jesus' words that no one comes to the Father except through Him? How would disbelief affect our identity? Our mission?

----

6 The founders or "holy men" of other religions often claim to speak for God. What is the difference between Jesus' teaching about God and other religious leaders' teaching about God? Why does the difference matter?

----

7 How is Jesus' claim to be the truth for everybody both exclusive ("the only truth") and inclusive ("for everyone")? How does this impact our mission?

----

8 What is the significance of Jesus' bodily resurrection for the Christian faith? How does Christ's work shine light on His claim to be the life?

----

9 If you were asked to list the three most important and unique aspects of Christianity, what would you choose? What separates Christianity from other religions?

----

10 Knowing that Jesus is the only Savior for all people, how should we think about global missions and taking the gospel to people of all types?

Part 2

THE BIG QUESTIONS

The fall of humanity into sin caused the corruption of God's creation, and this has led humanity to wrestle with some big questions in this life. Does life have meaning? Is God good? Why do we suffer? Is hell necessary? Only a God-centered worldview properly answers the deepest questions of our hearts.

Chapter 6

By Mary Jo Sharp

The Meaning of Life

Does Life Have Meaning Without God?

VOICES FROM *the Church*

"Modern man thought that when he had gotten rid of God, he had freed himself from all that repressed and stifled him. Instead, he discovered that in killing God, he had only succeeded in orphaning himself. For if there is no God, then man's life becomes absurd." [1]

–William Lane Craig

VOICES FROM *the Church*

"Death is the ultimate weapon of the tyrant; resurrection does not make a covenant with death, it overthrows it. The resurrection, in the full Jewish and early Christian sense, is the ultimate affirmation that creation matters, that embodied human beings matter." [2]

–N. T. Wright

Beginning in January of 2009, the British Humanist Society ran a bus advertising campaign touting this "reassuring" message, "There's probably no God. Now stop worrying and enjoy your life." The ad campaign was part of a project designed to brighten up the image of atheism, which traditionally has a gloomy feel of atheists grappling with the angst of a purposeless universe.

But more than merely creating a gloomy disposition, the atheistic view of the universe, as atheist philosopher Julian Baggini asserts, puts forth a view of reality that includes "no salvation, no redemption, no second chances. Lives can go terribly wrong in ways that can never be put right." [3]

This is the reality of a universe that is void of the Creator. Life is meaningless, and though atheists can live as though life has meaning, there is no real source of meaning.

In Ecclesiastes, Solomon wrote of his attempt to find meaning for life. He limited himself to human reasoning and only to that which can be found "under the sun." Solomon looked for purpose and meaning in a world void of God. His conclusion? Vanity of vanities; life is meaningless—if there is no God.

In this chapter, we will answer the skeptic who believes that life can have ultimate meaning apart from God. We will also show why the death and resurrection of Jesus is necessary for redemption, forgiveness, and meaning in this life. This study is for those who have struggled with or know others struggling with the question of God's existence and our purpose in this world.

Apart from God, there is no justice (Eccl. 3:16-20).

King Solomon was considered to be one of the wisest of all men in history. His wisdom is compared with the wisdom of the Egyptians (1 Kings 4:29-34) and was displayed in the example of the two prostitutes (1 Kings 3:16-28). Because of his great wisdom, Solomon knew that apart from God, all human wisdom and effort is meaningless.

As Solomon looked for meaning in the world, he considered how people treated one another. He imagined a world without God's justice in the afterlife. When Solomon looked out into the world, he found wickedness everywhere. He argued that God would eventually judge all persons, the righteous and the unrighteous. He couldn't help but note in Ecclesiastes 3:16-20 that apart from God, man is no better than the beasts.

16 I also observed under the sun: there is wickedness at the place of judgment and there is wickedness at the place of righteousness. 17 I said to myself, "God will judge the righteous and the wicked, since there is a time for every activity and every work." 18 I said to myself, "This happens concerning people, so that God may test them and they may see for themselves that they are like animals." 19 For the fate of people and the fate of animals is the same. As one dies, so dies the other; they all have the same breath. People have no advantage over animals since everything is futile. 20 All are going to the same place; all come from dust, and all return to dust.

Without justice from God, mankind's actions can't be considered as better or worse than those of the beasts. Solomon's reasoning for this conclusion was because in the end, we all go to the same end—death and the end of our existence (v. 20).

As Christian philosopher William Lane Craig notes, "If life ends at the grave, then it makes no difference whether one has lived as a Stalin or as a saint. Since one's destiny is ultimately unrelated to one's behavior, you may as well just live as you please." [4]

If God ultimately judges human beings, it means that humans are the sort of being that is worthy of being judged. Do you see? The idea of judgment assumes that people are responsible and important, that their actions have real consequences.

In our society, we reflect this idea through our court system. People are brought to trial because it is assumed they are capable of responsibility for their actions. Therefore, they are judged accordingly.

Conversely, the absence of God's judgment upon mankind would suggest that we are not responsible beings, no more responsible than animals. We could rape and murder or nurture and love, but in the end, nothing would be of any consequence.

Solomon described the situation that would follow as "absolute futility"— all life becomes meaningless. If there is no judgment for humanity, then human life is of no consequence, and furthermore, human life has no meaning. This was the same conclusion to which some modern atheist philosophers arrived— all was meaningless.

If our existence has no ultimate meaning, then as the apostle Paul stated in 1 Corinthians 15:32, it would seem best to "eat and drink, for tomorrow we die." But for many people, the idea that our lives make no difference whatsoever can result in hopelessness and despair.

When I was an older teenager, I remember one particularly bad day in which I ended up in tears, curled up in a ball on my bedroom floor. The thought that kept running through my mind was: *How foolish it was to think that my feelings mattered in a vast universe where individual humans were only a speck of dust on a relatively insignificant, small planet.* I wondered why anyone should actually care about me and what reasons I had for thinking my life mattered. At that time, I was still essentially an atheist. I began to realize that I would live and die and that was all there is—my life ultimately did not matter. The idea that there is no justice is the logical conclusion of a worldview that has no place for God.

Apart from God, there is no good or evil (Eccl. 4:1-3).

Removing God as Creator not only removes ultimate meaning and purpose from which mankind derives values, but it also entails removal of the grounding for what we call *evil*. Evil becomes just a part of everything "under the sun." However, evil is something we all comprehend and experience. Let's look at Solomon's conclusion about life if there is no God.

1 *Again, I observed all the acts of oppression being done under the sun. Look at the tears of those who are oppressed; they have no one to comfort them. Power is with those who oppress them; they have no one to comfort them.* 2 *So I admired the dead, who have already died, more than the living, who are still alive.* 3 *But better than either of them is the one who has not yet existed, who has not seen the evil activity that is done under the sun.*

Solomon examined the oppressed. He noted that there is none to comfort them in their oppression. If there is no Comforter, the oppressed suffer, and that's just the way things are.

Here again, Solomon finds injustice under the sun. Those with power abuse their position, causing pain to those they oppress.

On this issue, King Solomon and atheist philosopher Friedrich Nietzsche seemed to understand the same truth from different perspectives: in a universe void of God, there is no authority for establishing what is good and evil. Those with power do as they please. Because Solomon believed in God, he found this to be a predicament that is grossly unjust. Nietzche, an atheist, found that there is no predicament but only a description of life instead.

Solomon's final conclusion was that it would be better never to exist in a world without God due to the amount of evil and suffering under the sun!

He argued that our very existence is absurd and futile without an ultimate answer to the great evil he saw in the world. Some scholars believe this statement is hyperbolic, intending to catch the reader's attention. However, Solomon's message comes across clearly whether hyperbolic or not. There is so much oppression in this world that people can question whether or not it is better to exist if this is all there is.

This problem of evil referenced by Solomon is also one of the most frequent objections to the existence of God. C. S. Lewis once was an atheist because he believed the universe to be "cruel and unjust." But over time, he realized that the existence of good and evil was pointing toward God, not away from Him.

Lewis wrote: "How had I got this idea of just and unjust? A man does not call a line crooked unless he has some idea of a straight line. What was I comparing this universe with when I called it unjust? If the whole show was bad and senseless from A to Z, so to speak, why did I, who was supposed to be part of the show, find myself in such violent reaction against it? A man feels wet when he falls into water, because man is not a water animal: a fish would not feel wet. Of course I could have given up my idea of justice by saying it was nothing but a private idea of my own. But if I did that, then my argument against God collapsed too—for the argument depended on saying that the world was really unjust, not simply that it did not happen to please my fancies. Thus in the very act of trying to prove that God did not exist—in other words, that the whole of reality was senseless—I found I was forced to assume that one part of reality— namely my idea of justice—was full of sense. Consequently atheism turns out to be too simple. If the whole universe has no meaning, we should never have found out that it has no meaning: just as, if there were no light in the universe and therefore no creatures with eyes, we should never know it was dark. Dark would be a word without meaning."[5]

Christ's resurrection gives us meaning and a mission (1 Cor. 15:12-19).

One of the most important ways God has communicated that human life has meaning, value, and purpose was through the work of Jesus in His death and resurrection. In the Christian view, "God does exist, and man's life does not end at the grave."[6]

Take a look at what Paul claimed about the resurrection in 1 Corinthians 15:12-19:

12 *Now if Christ is proclaimed as raised from the dead, how can some of you say, "There is no resurrection of the dead"?* 13 *But if there is no resurrection of the dead, then Christ has not been raised;* 14 *and if Christ has not been raised, then our proclamation is without foundation, and so is your faith.* 15 *In addition, we are found to be false witnesses about God, because we have testified about God that He raised up Christ—whom He did not raise up if in fact the dead are not raised.* 16 *For if the dead are not raised, Christ has not been raised.* 17 *And if Christ has not been raised, your faith is worthless; you are still in your sins.* 18 *Therefore, those who have fallen asleep in Christ have also perished.* 19 *If we have put our hope in Christ for this life only, we should be pitied more than anyone.*

In this passage, Paul emphasized the connection between an actual resurrection, faith in God, and forgiveness of sin. He began by saying that if there is no actual resurrection of the dead, then the faith we've placed in Jesus is useless, vain, without foundation. Remember Solomon's findings on the meaning of life if there is no God? He found all to be in vain, "absolute futility." In a similar thought, if there is no resurrection of the dead, then our hope in Jesus is just "absolute futility"—meaningless.

Notice the importance the apostle Paul placed on the absolute reality of the resurrection. Jesus must have physically risen from the dead for our faith to be worth anything. Why? The object of our faith must be worthy of that faith.

For example, it wouldn't make much sense for me to place my faith in a chair with broken legs, no matter how much I wished it to be worthy of my faith. The reality is that if the chair is not worthy, I cannot trust it to hold me up. So if Jesus didn't actually rise from the dead, then He is not worthy of our trust.

Interestingly enough, Paul not only emphasized the reality of Jesus' historical resurrection, but he also focused on what the resurrection means for humankind. Look back at verse 17. Paul explained that if Christ hasn't been raised from the dead, we are still in our sins. This statement reminds us of what Julian Baggini, the atheist philosopher, asserted, that in an atheistic worldview, there is "no salvation, no redemption, no second chances. Lives can go terribly wrong in ways that can never be put right."[7]

This is the reality we must face in a universe void of a Savior—no possibility of redemption. Without the resurrection of Jesus as an actual event of history, we have no Redeemer for our sins. There is no place to ground real redemption.

When we hurt people, destroy lives, inflict pain, we carry these "sins" with us the rest of our lives. Then we die. We must acknowledge that the only responsible reaction to our situation of hopelessness in such a universe is Bertrand Russell's "unyielding despair."[8]

The source of the redemption that is possible is found in the historical resurrection of Jesus. "But now Christ has been raised from the dead, the firstfruits of those who have fallen asleep" (1 Cor. 15:20). How does the resurrection of Jesus provide for our salvation, our redemption, our second chance? Through the defeat of death: "For since death came through a man, the resurrection of the dead also comes through a man. For as in Adam all die, so also in Christ all will be made alive. But each in his own order: Christ, the firstfruits; afterward, at His coming, those who belong to Christ. Then comes the end, when He hands over the kingdom to God the Father, when He abolishes all rule and all authority and power. For He must reign until He puts all His enemies under His feet. The last enemy to be abolished is death" (vv. 21-26). This is a crucial point in handling the problem of meaning, value, and purpose in human lives.

In the atheist view of the universe, death comes equally to everything. Just as we all enter the world without meaning or purpose, we end without meaning or purpose. Death is simply the end of "me." I have no reward or punishment, no consequences. I do whatever I will, and then I die.

In the Christian view, death is an enemy because it is a result of evil. In accordance with Romans 6:23, "the wages of sin is death." Death is the consequence of our sin. Yet for our sin to have a consequence, it has to have meaning. For our sin to have meaning, it must come from creatures who are infused with meaning. Jesus' death to pay the wages of sin evidences that our sin has a consequence and therefore our lives have meaning. His resurrection, defeating the enemy of death, evidences that our lives are valuable and worth redeeming. Yet if all is meaninglessness, nothing has meaning—neither our sin nor our own lives.

It's a double standard to want your life to be infused with meaning and purpose but want your sin to be meaningless and insignificant. If it is true that we have meaning and purpose, then so do our thoughts and actions.

Instead of leaving us to our fate of death and destruction, instead of declaring us a cosmic orphan, God redeems His good creation because it has value. This is not value that can be obtained by accident, arising out of a purposeless universe. Being the creation of God means that you and I were intentionally made. We each have purpose.

The worth of a human is shown beautifully through Jesus' teaching. He described the Creator of the universe—the kind of Being who can make powerful stars such as our sun—as knowing the number of hairs on your head. If God knows each and every sparrow (a bird of relative insignificance in Jesus' day), then how much more does He know about and care about you, the one made in His own image (Gen. 1:27)?

Conclusion

As I mentioned earlier, I was an atheist who began to wonder if my life had any meaning or value. I couldn't find a reason for thinking that it did if I was just a speck of atoms in a vast, indifferent universe. The lack of a basis for meaning and purpose to human life in an atheistic worldview was one thing that drove me to consider that there may be a God.

If there is a God who created me, then there must have been a reason for my creation since it was intentional and not accidental. If there is no God, then I am an accident of the universe and my creation has no reason. I have to accept these basic tenets in order to properly consider both views. However, the first view of a Creator fits with the understanding that humans have value, meaning, and purpose.

Hymn of *Response*

Love divine, all loves excelling, Joy of heav'n to earth come down;
Fix in us Thy humble dwelling; All Thy faithful mercies crown.
Jesus, Thou art all compassion, Pure, unbounded love Thou art;
Visit us with Thy salvation; Enter ev'ry trembling heart.

Finish, then, Thy new creation; Pure and spotless let us be;
Let us see Thy great salvation Perfectly restored in Thee:
Changed from glory into glory, Till in heav'n we take our place,
Till we cast our crowns before Thee, Lost in wonder, love and praise.
–Charles Wesley

Devotions

DISBELIEVING GOD HAS CONSEQUENCES

I've had many conversations with atheists over the years. Most of them look solely at what I will call "physical evidence." They want to see God's footprint on the ground or a cross of shining stars in the sky (the latter as stated by Carl Sagan, the host of the old science show *Cosmos*). While I do discuss the physical evidence with them from God's general revelation, I always try to push them further. We must also consider the consequences of a worldview that says there is no God because there are consequences.

When King Solomon decided to look at the world apart from God, he gave us an unexpected glimpse into the heart of an atheistic worldview. He gave us some insight into the costs of disbelieving in God—all is meaningless. Everything that goes on "under the sun" is without ultimate purpose or meaning. This is a result of disbelief in God.

Take a moment to read Romans 1:28-31, where Paul lists the end results for mankind when men turn away from God. An atheist might say, "But that's not what always happens. I'm not like that!" Though it is true that individuals can still act morally without believing in God, there is no reason for why they should act morally. This lack of moral liability, resulting from disbelief in God, has broad sweeping consequences for mankind.

As you prepare to encounter Solomon's examination of a world void of God, allow God to show you how your beliefs affect your own life, the lives of the ones you love, and how they can potentially affect the world

Pause and Reflect

1   Why should we consider the consequences of our beliefs?

- -

2   What are some ramifications of disbelief in God? What are some ramifications of belief in God?

- -

3   What would other people say about your belief in God as they observe your life and interact with you?

Longing for Meaning

Everyone everywhere wants his or her life to be filled with meaning. The grave thought of my life entailing absolute purposelessness would ultimately lead me to bitter despair. Yet how do we establish that our lives actually have meaning? Where do we get the grounding to establish meaning and/or purpose?

A house needs a solid foundation in order for it to stand firm. When a person attempts to sell a house, they usually have trouble if the foundation is cracked or unstable. It is equally important to establish a foundation for the structural soundness of the belief that our individual lives have meaning and purpose.

Jesus taught that a firm foundation is built on belief in God. He didn't teach this as one alternative to many others. He taught it as the only structurally sound option. Take a moment to read the parable of the two builders in Matthew 7:24-27.

How great a collapse we will experience when we try to live our lives on structurally unsound beliefs! Think of all the fruitless efforts of chasing after things we believe will give us meaning and purpose in life that will fail us due to faulty foundations. Think of the times that this chasing has caused us to hurt someone else during our pursuit.

God is the grounding for meaning and purpose because He purposefully created us! God is the only trustworthy foundation because He is perfectly good. Remember the problem with the house foundation? It cannot be trusted if it is not perfectly good. The same thing is true for finding meaning and purpose somewhere outside of a perfectly good foundation—it cannot be trusted.

Pause and Reflect

1   Jesus described a house built on the rock versus a house built on the sand. What was the difference?

---

2   How does a firm foundation stabilize a structure?

---

3   How does a firm foundation in God stabilize our belief that our lives are infused with meaning and purpose?

Asking Good Questions

Christians spend a lot of time answering questions and not enough asking questions. In order to effectively help others see truth, we may also have to help them break through some poor reasoning and dogmatic presuppositions. Some examples of good questions to ask when you hear a statement about belief in God are (1) What do you mean by that? (2) How do you know that? (aka Where are you getting that from?) and (3) Why do you believe that?

The first question helps the other person discover what the statement means. Never assume that a person knows what they are talking about! Likewise, you are better equipped to answer someone else if you are actually addressing what the person believes and not what you assume is believed.

The second and third questions aid both people in the conversation in understanding the source of the information and why that source is trusted as an authority. In the argument that human life is meaningful and valuable, I've heard the source authority as the social agreement of the human community that human beings have value. Do you see a problem with this source? It places human beings (and typically those in power) with the ultimate authority on human value. In our recent history, we humans have defined some humans as *not human* in order to strip them of their value and use them as we please (ex. antebellum slavery).

Asking questions is first and foremost a way to help us better minister to others. Challenging untruths is a part of loving people, but it must be done in a way that demonstrates a sincere love for them. It can never be done in a mean spirit that seeks simply to "win an argument" and "zing" an unbeliever.

Pause and Reflect

1   Can you think of any Scriptures in which Jesus effectively broke down a person's wrong beliefs in order to show them the truth?

- -

2   How can you ask questions about a person's beliefs without coming across as rude or aggressive?

- -

3   Ask God to put people in your path with whom you can have some great discussions about the "big questions" in life.

DISCUSSION QUESTIONS

1   In what ways is the question of the existence of God important to finding meaning and purpose for life? Why is the question of meaning and purpose important for people to ask?

----

2   What do you think about atheists undertaking a publicity campaign to improve the image of atheism? Why do you think atheism struggles with image problems?

----

3   What do you think Solomon referred to when he observed wickedness in the place of righteousness (Eccl. 3:16)? What does he say of mankind?

----

4   What are some problems that arise when people are absolved of responsibility for their actions? How does failure to hold people accountable diminish the value of human life?

----

5   What are the implications of a universe void of God? Have you ever thought to question a skeptical friend's belief that there is no God on the basis of meaning and purpose?

----

6   What does Solomon say in Ecclesiastes 4:1-3 about the oppressed versus the oppressors? What does Solomon conclude about life in light of the amount and extent of great evil "under the sun"?

----

7   How would you respond to someone who claims that evil disproves the existence of God?

----

8   If there is no God, then the great evils that we find objectionable are just the way the world is "under the sun." In what ways does believing in God provide us with the tools to distinguish right from wrong?

----

9   How would you respond to the person who says the Christian faith doesn't depend on Christ being physically raised from the dead? What does Paul claim about Christianity in 1 Corinthians 15 if there is no resurrection?

----

10   How does the caring nature of God impact the way we think about our mission as Christians? In what ways does our view of human value reinforce our efforts to share the gospel?

Chapter 7

By Christian George

The Character of God

Is God Good?

"God is good, all the time. All the time, God is good." But is He really? Critics of Christianity point to puzzling passages that seem to show God as angry or bigoted. If they can prove the Bible portrays a racist, vengeful God, then they can strike at the heart of Christianity's central claim—that God is good and loving.

Atheist Richard Dawkins, in *The God Delusion,* once described God this way: "The God of the Old Testament is arguably the most unpleasant character in all fiction: jealous and proud of it; a petty, unjust, unforgiving control-freak; a vindictive, bloodthirsty ethnic cleanser; a misogynistic, homophobic, racist, infanticidal, genocidal, filicidal, pestilential, megalomaniacal, sadomasochistic, capriciously malevolent bully."[3]

Putting Dawkins' hyperbole aside, we must recognize the existence of multiple texts that show God as angry over sin or jealous for His people. This predicament pushes us into deeper questions. Can God be angry and loving at the same time? Can God choose a special people (in this case, Israel) and yet still love everyone in the world?

In this chapter, we will look at the goodness of God through the lens of His dealings with the Canaanites. By exploring God's command to wipe out the Canaanites in the Old Testament, we will address the question "Is God angry?" By exploring Jesus' interaction with a Canaanite woman in the New Testament, we will address the question "Is God racist?"

The goal of this chapter is to provide a defense against those who claim that God is by nature violent and bigoted by examining how God's holiness and patience reveal His goodness in the blessing of His people and all people.

Is God angry? The holiness of God reveals His goodness in the blessing of His people (Deut. 7:1-5).

Is God angry? To answer this question properly, we must recognize that there are two types of anger—sinful anger and righteous anger.

The sinful anger you and I often feel comes from a place of selfishness, entitlement, jealousy, and stubbornness. It says, "I deserve to be treated better!" and "Who are you to say that about me?" As self-centered creatures, we elevate ourselves so high that when someone cuts us down, whether through words or actions, it creates within us a hostile and violent reaction.

But righteous anger is altogether different. Righteous anger comes from a different place, a godly place. It's what you experience when you witness injustice in the world. When the weak, the helpless, the vulnerable, the voiceless are abused. Anger over injustice is an emotion that is more than just okay; it's commanded in Scripture. Only in our anger, we must avoid sinning. Paul put it simply, "Be angry and do not sin" (Eph. 4:26).

It's not just Christians who experience anger; God gets angry too. What provokes God to righteous anger? Let's take a look at one of the passages often cited as problematic for those of us who believe God is good. In Deuteronomy 7:1-5, Moses lays out the strict guidelines for purging the promised land of its inhabitants:

> 1 *"When the LORD your God brings you into the land you are entering to possess, and He drives out many nations before you—the Hittites, Girgashites, Amorites, Canaanites, Perizzites, Hivites and Jebusites, seven nations more numerous and powerful than you—* 2 *and when the LORD your God delivers them over to you and you defeat them, you must completely destroy them. Make no treaty with them and show them no mercy.* 3 *Do not intermarry with them. Do not give your daughters to their sons or take their daughters for your sons,* 4 *because they will turn your sons away from Me to worship other gods. Then the LORD's anger will burn against you, and He will swiftly destroy you.* 5 *Instead, this is what you are to do to them: tear down their altars, smash their sacred pillars, cut down their Asherah poles, and burn up their carved images.*

Let's set this passage in context. The Israelites were on the move. They had crossed the Red Sea, wandered in the wilderness, and now, after 40 years of going in circles, were finally entering the promised land. But there was a problem. The land was full of pagans: the Amorites, Girgashites, Canaanites, and a number of other "ites." In order to obey God and enjoy the blessing of His promise to Abraham, the Israelites needed to conquer these people. So God gave them a "take no prisoners" set of instructions on how to do it. But how could a loving God give this kind of instruction? Doesn't God care about them?

Innocent or Guilty?

First, we need to recognize that the people of Canaan were anything but innocent. In fact, they were exceedingly evil (see Gen. 15:16; Lev. 18:25; Deut. 9:5). The gods they worshiped demanded human sacrifices, and the Canaanites offered them in droves. You want grain? You want rain? Then you must sacrifice your sons and daughters. To appease the god Molech, for instance, the Ammonites took their newly born screaming infants and threw them into the fire.

Not only did the Canaanites practice infanticide, they were also notorious for their cruelty and immorality. Bestiality, rape, molestation, and other sexual sins abounded in full force (Lev. 18–20). Sorcery, incantations, fortune telling— all were commonplace in Canaan (Deut. 18:9-14).

And as if the Canaanites could not degenerate any further, they participated in one of the most unnatural, repulsive acts any human could do to another—they feasted on the flesh of their enemies. Have you ever wondered where the word *cannibal* came from? You guessed it—Canaan. [4] So when we talk about God's command to utterly wipe these peoples off the map, we must first recognize that the Canaanites were exceedingly and unapologetically socially and spiritually wicked.

Slow to Anger

Second, God gave the Canaanites opportunities to repent. As cruel and devious as they were—as horrendous and loathsome as the Canaanites proved themselves to be—the forgiveness of God was not beyond their grasp.

How odd of God! That He should extend His love even to those who constantly provoked Him to wrath. Would you? Listen to what God told Jonah: "Is it right for you to be angry?...Should I not care about the great city of Nineveh, which has more than 120,000 people?" (Jonah 4:4,11). God never took pleasure in ordering the death of the Canaanites: "Do I take any pleasure in the death of the wicked?...Instead, don't I take pleasure when he turns from his ways and lives?" (Ezek. 18:23).

The Israelites themselves often provoked God to wrath. From the time they left Egypt, they were a bunch of complainers and whiners. Of course, when they constructed a golden calf, the anger of God burned hotly against them. He wanted to destroy them on the spot. But Moses pleaded fiercely on behalf of his people: "Turn from Your great anger and relent concerning this disaster planned for Your people" (Ex. 32:12).

Which He did. And that's just the thing about God. His inclination is to forgive. Instead of wiping out His rebellious people, God forgave them. Patient, longsuffering, instinctively compassionate—that's the God of the Hebrews. Isaiah got it right: "I will praise You, LORD, although You were angry with me. Your anger has turned away, and You have had compassion on me" (Isa. 12:1).

When Judgment Comes

Eventually, however, the patience of God ran out. If the Canaanites had repented, God would have lovingly spared them. But now, punishment was on its way. Judgment day had arrived for the Canaanites, and eventually for the Israelites who adopted their pagan practices.

God's holiness always demands justice. It demanded justice in the Canaanites, and it also demanded justice in the Israelites.

The love of God does not negate the justice of God. As the prophet acknowledged, "Your eyes are too pure to look on evil" (Hab. 1:13). If the Israelites left the Canaanites alive, they would be tempted to marry into their families and give their daughters to the sons of the Canaanites. In doing so, they would abandon the worship of God and adopt the practices and rituals of the pagan peoples.

Which is exactly what happened. The Israelites did not wipe out all of the Canaanites. Because the Israelites married into these cultures, they adopted their practices and set up Asherah poles. They worshiped Baal and other gods. They even sacrificed their own children to appease Molech (2 Kings 17:17; 23:10). Moreover, they began to do the unthinkable. They began to eat their offspring just like their cannibal neighbors (see 2 Kings 6:29; Deut. 28:53).

Is God a moral monster? No. Without God, we are the moral monsters! We are the creatures that contaminated creation, the ones who provoke a holy and just God to righteous anger. "I was an unthinking animal toward You," the psalmist correctly confessed (Ps. 73:22). The anger of God is His right reaction to evil. But the love of God and the compassion of God will exist long after evil is annihilated. Long after sin and anger are abolished, love will remain.

Listen to what God told Isaiah: "In a surge of anger I hid My face from you for a moment, but I will have compassion on you with everlasting love" (Isa. 54:8). The love of God is more than a mere emotion. It is God's most fundamental and self-defining trait. It goes to the very core of God's being. It's part of His deepest DNA. For "God is love" (1 John 4:8).

We come to the Bible and admit we don't understand everything about God. We still have questions. We are not alone. It was Christ who raised His own question mark as He was raised on the wooden pole: "My God, My God, why have You forsaken Me" (Matt. 27:46). It was a question that has a magnificent answer—the blessing that God offers His people is the sacrifice of His one and only Son.

At the cross, the question shifts from "Is God angry?" to "Is God angry forever?" With a heartfelt hope experienced by all of God's people throughout history, we can confidently exclaim no! Because of Christ's work, a day is coming when that which makes God angry—and that which makes us angry—will forever be forgotten. Sin will be no more. Death will die. No more holocausts, famine, or war. As God Himself said, "It is I who sweep away your transgressions for My own sake and remember your sins no more" (Isa. 43:25).

Is God racist? The plan of God reveals His goodness in the blessing of all people (Matt. 15:21-28).

Is God racist? In one search engine, this question generated 40,000 responses. It's a question all serious students of the Bible must grapple with. In this section, we will tackle this accusation head on by looking at a passage in the New Testament that some believe smacks of racism—Christ's interaction with the Canaanite woman.

But we discover that this is a story about grace, not race. Whereas Jesus came first for the Jews, His patience is revealed in how He uses the Jews to bless all nations and races. Let's take a closer look at our passage:

21 *When Jesus left there, He withdrew to the area of Tyre and Sidon.* 22 *Just then a Canaanite woman from that region came and kept crying out, "Have mercy on me, Lord, Son of David! My daughter is cruelly tormented by a demon."*

23 *Yet He did not say a word to her. So His disciples approached Him and urged Him, "Send her away because she cries out after us."*

24 *He replied, "I was sent only to the lost sheep of the house of Israel."*

25 *But she came, knelt before Him, and said, "Lord, help me!"*

26 *He answered, "It isn't right to take the children's bread and throw it to their dogs."*

27 *"Yes, Lord," she said, "yet even the dogs eat the crumbs that fall from their masters' table!"*

28 *Then Jesus replied to her, "Woman, your faith is great. Let it be done for you as you want." And from that moment her daughter was cured.*

It's not everyday that God calls someone a dog. Only one time in the Bible does Jesus speak to a woman to this degree. We don't know much about this woman. Only that she was a Canaanite—a descendant of the cannibalistic, child-sacrificing nations that God once commanded His people to destroy. We know her daughter was possessed by a demon. And like any mother desperate to see her child healed, she fought her way to Jesus and exclaimed, "Have mercy on me, Lord, Son of David!" (v. 22).

Jesus said His ministry was to the Jewish people, not the Canaanites: "It isn't right to take the children's bread and throw it to their dogs" (v. 26). In essence, He was saying it is wrong to take what rightfully belongs to the Jews and give it to the Canaanites.

It is here that the story takes an unexpected turn. Instead of contradicting Christ, the woman agreed with Him: "Yes, Lord, if you say I'm a dog, I'm a dog. But even the dogs eat the crumbs that fall from their masters' table!" What boldness!

Talk about sassing the Savior! This was a daring, dogged kind of faith that Jesus rarely saw even in His own disciples. "Woman," He said to her, "your faith is great, let it be done for you as you want" (v. 28). Does this passage suggest that God is racist? Some say yes. But it's important to recognize that Jesus came first and foremost for the Jews (Matt. 10:5-6; John 4:22; Rom. 1:16).

In the Old Testament, God selected the Jews to be His particular people, a nation through which He would accomplish His saving purposes. While He lavished His love on anyone who believed—the Canaanites, Ninevites, and any other "ites" who turned from their wicked ways—His plan had always been (1) to choose the Jews and (2) to use the Jews for the blessing of all nations.

In the New Testament, Jesus modeled the same principle. Born a Jew, raised a Jew, Jesus preached in Jewish synagogues (Matt. 4:23) and observed Jewish festivals (John 5:1). All of Christ's disciples were Jews. He would later send apostles and disciples to evangelize the Gentiles. But while He walked the earth, Christ's message was intended first for one people—the Jews. Jerusalem first, then the very ends of the earth. That was the evangelistic strategy of Jesus Christ.

But every once in a while, Jesus foreshadowed the future, injecting the future into the present. Like the time He had to travel through Samaria to minister to a Samaritan woman. Like the times He healed Gentiles or ministered to people who worked for the Roman Empire.

Consistently in His ministry, Jesus showed that grace triumphs over race. The fact that Jesus was traveling through Tyre and Sidon reveals His interest in the salvation of other nations (v. 21). That's why at the end of His earthly ministry, He commanded His disciples to "make disciples of all nations" (Matt. 28:19). Paul later wrote, "There is no Jew or Greek, slave or free, male or female; for you are all one in Christ Jesus" (Gal. 3:28).

Think about Abraham, looking into the Milky Way heavens as God promised to make his descendants as numerous as the stippled sky (Gen. 26:4). Through God's patience with the Jews, He would bless all nations. Through His patience in even listening to the Canaanite woman, He proved a point to His disciples—that although Christ came first for the Jews, the Jews would reject Christ. And then people from every tribe and nation would be included in the grand drama of redemption.

Genealogies, seemingly boring, also hold the answer to our question "Is God racist?" Remember the Canaanite prostitute Rahab, who assisted the Israelites in capturing the city of Jericho (Josh. 6:17)? Because of Rahab's bold faith, her life and those of her family were spared from the judgment. Moreover, God valued Rahab's actions so much that she became an ancestor to none other than Jesus Christ Himself (Matt. 1:5)—a significant branch in God's family tree.

Like her ancestor of long before, the Canaanite woman in our passage exposed a fundamental truth about the love and goodness of God—whoever believes in Christ can be saved, regardless of race, regardless of nationality. It doesn't matter who you are, or where you're from, or where you've been, or what you've done.

Though some passages in the Bible seem to smack of racism and have been used in history to justify horrendous crimes, the accusation that God is racist just doesn't hold water. The argument is thin as soup. Jesus never rejected anyone for his or her nationality. In fact, the opposite is true. Christ sent His disciples to all places to proclaim the goodness of His gospel. As Peter confessed, "God doesn't show favoritism, but in every nation the person who fears Him and does righteousness is acceptable to Him" (Acts 10:34-35).

One day, at the great banquet feast of heaven, people from every tribe, tongue, and nation will sit down for a meal (Luke 14:15-24). They will not eat as dogs, lapping up the crumbs that fall from the Master's table. They will not eat as slaves or foreigners but instead as children of the Most High. As heirs of God and co-heirs with Christ, they will dine in perfect fellowship with the God who loves, the God who is good.

Conclusion

The ultimate answer to the question "Is God good?" must necessarily resolve in the cross and resurrection of Jesus Christ. Yes, God is good. And not just good, He's great! Death defeated, sin crucified, God is in the process of reversing the effects of the fall. Through the ministry of the church, He's setting right all the wrongs in the world. Where there is murder, He gives life. Where there is despair, hope. That's the Yahweh way! And God will not tolerate sin in this world much longer.

So be on the lookout! Christ is putting back together what has been broken—humpty-dumpty style. Stitching together what is splintered. Gluing together what is fractured. Nothing is too damaged. No one is too shattered. This is the hope of humanity, the triumph of the cross. The re-creation of God's creation is the ultimate gospel project.

For this reason, you and I can continue proclaiming the reasons for the hope that we have in Christ. The big debates will always exist, but through the power of the Scripture and the promise of the Spirit, we can continue hammering some of the most difficult question marks in the Bible into exclamation points—ones that point upward to God's grace, glory, and eternal goodness.

Devotions

THE REALLY LONG NOSE OF GOD

Noses come in all shapes and sizes. Some are thin, others wide. Some are twisted, others pointed. We even change our noses. On average, Americans receive an average of 50,000 cosmetic nose jobs every year. [5]

Did you know that God has a really long nose? An English translation of Exodus 34:6 says, "Yahweh—Yahweh is a compassionate and gracious God, slow to anger and rich in faithful love and truth." But in Hebrew, "slow to anger" literally reads "the long-nosed One."

Why would God have a long nose? Because He's patient. Length here refers to time—minutes, not inches. It took a long time for God's nose to grow red. The Israelites knew it. It took a lot of complaining in the desert and a lot of idolatry in Canaan to set God off. His nose was long, not because He lies (as in the fairy tale *Pinocchio*) but because He loves. That's why throughout the Old Testament, God's response is slow to anger.

What's yours? Are you patient or short-tempered? Snappy or long-nosed? How would your friends describe you? Your siblings? Your spouse? Can others smell the fruit of the Spirit on you? Love, joy, peace, patience (Gal. 5:22)? God's nose is long, and ours should be also.

Pause and Reflect

1   Why is patience such a difficult attribute to cultivate?

2   What three things require the most patience from you?

3   Anger is not an end in itself. What other sins has anger generated in your life? What is the ultimate solution to anger?

Falling Up

Sometimes we've got to go back in order to go forward.

Leave your car keys in the house? Gotta go back and get them. Miss an exit on the interstate? Turn that car around. Most of us hate backtracking. We were made to go forward! Our knees bend forward. Our face points forward. Sure, some of us might have eyes in the back of our head, but as a whole, we are forward-leaning creatures.

Paul wrote, "If anyone is in Christ, he is a new creation; old things have passed away, and look, new things have come" (2 Cor. 5:17). In other words, Christians live in reverse. We are going back in order to go forward. Back to Eden. Back to our pre-fallen state. Back to the time when God walked with humans in the cool of the day (Gen. 3:8). Through the process of sanctification, we are being restored to what we were originally intended to be.

In Adam, all of us fell into sin (Rom. 5:12). But since Christ overcame sin, we are now falling forward…and upward. Since we have been raised with Christ, we can set our thoughts on things above (Col. 3:1). Off of the things of this world. Off of the Canaanite attractions that daily seek to steal our attention. Off of the idols of our age—the gods of greed, unhealthy ambition, and entertainment. Redemption is the way forward. And all of us are falling for something. The question becomes "What are you falling for?"

Pause and Reflect

1   What are the barriers keeping you from becoming like Christ in your thoughts? Actions? Attitudes?

----

2   Reflect on the following statement: Decrease is more precious to Yahweh than increase. Do you agree with this? Why or why not?

----

3   In the past few days, how have you witnessed the goodness of God in your life?

FROM RACISM TO GRACISM

Technically, there is only one race—the human race. Sure, there are different expressions of our race—Semitic, Chinese, Polynesian, African, Caucasian, and so forth. But as a whole, we all share 99.99+ percent of the same genetic makeup.

Jesus came to earth for the human race. Aren't you glad He didn't come for the angels (Heb. 2:16)? For the plants? And as much as we love our pets, Jesus didn't hang on the cross for the transgressions of Snowball, Fluffy, or Rex the Hamster.

True enough, God has plans to redeem creation (Rom. 8:19-21), and He will create a new heaven and a new earth (Rev. 21:1). But it was for you that God's arms were outstretched on the cross. It was for your sins that Christ absorbed with full sensitivity the awful wrath of God.

That's why we can sing the children's song without crossing our fingers: "Red and yellow, black and white, they are precious in His sight." No two people are truly identical—even identical twins are remarkably different. Yet all of us are part of the same global family, a world that God loved so much that He sacrificed His only Son (John 3:16).

So let me ask you a question. If peoples from every tribe, tongue, and nation will live unified forever in heaven (Rev. 7:9), why do our churches here on earth appear so segregated, divided, and schismatic?

Pause and Reflect

1   Why does racism pose one of the greatest threats to evangelism?

----

2   Why is grace an effective answer to racism? What spiritual gifts are effective in overcoming racism?

----

3   Read John 17:21. What should this teach us about God's perspective of the church? How should this motivate us in our dealings with other denominations and Christian traditions?

DISCUSSION QUESTIONS

1   In what ways has the media portrayed God as vengeful, angry, or eager to destroy? Can you think of a movie or sitcom that portrays Christians as cruel, intolerant, or bigoted?

------

2   Have you encountered skeptics who use difficult Old Testament passages to explain their rejection of God? How would you respond to the claim that the God of the Bible is not "good"?

------

3   When was the last time you experienced righteous anger? What provokes you the most to this type of anger? How can a deeper knowledge of the holiness of God transform sinful anger into righteous anger?

------

4   How is the vision of God's compassion and judgment in the Old Testament similar to or different from the New Testament's depiction of Jesus?

------

5   What does it mean to be holy? Why was God so concerned about preserving the holiness of His people? In what ways did God attempt to keep His people holy?

------

6   Why is it good to recognize that we do not understand everything about God? In what ways can we keep our limited understanding from chipping away at our confidence in the character of God as He has revealed Himself to us?

------

7   Why do you think Jesus focused His earthly ministry on the Jewish people? How does taking into consideration the Bible's grand story line help you answer this difficult question?

------

8   What kinds of racism have you experienced or witnessed? What sin lies at the heart of racism?

------

9   Take a moment to read 1 Corinthians 12:12-13 and Colossians 3:11. How do these passages challenge the accusation that God is racist?

------

10 In what ways does the future vision of a banqueting table set for people from all nations impact our evangelistic strategies? How does the loving heart of God for all people motivate our mission efforts?

Chapter 8

By Michael Kelley

Suffering

Why Do We Suffer?

VOICES FROM *the Church*

"If we again ask the question: 'Why does God allow evil and suffering to continue?' and we look at the cross of Jesus, we still do not know what the answer is. However, we now know what the answer isn't. It can't be that he doesn't love us. It can't be that he is indifferent or detached from our condition. God takes our misery and suffering so seriously that he was willing to take it on himself."[1]
–Tim Keller

VOICES FROM *Church History*

"If some of you are passing just now through very trying providences, I pray with all my heart that they may be sanctified to you. It will be no ill wind which wrecks your ship, if the tempest casts you upon the Rock of Ages. I trust that the Lord is laying you low that he may build you up upon a sure foundation."[2]
–Charles Spurgeon (1834-1892)

Suffering is where the theological rubber meets the road. We might be well-educated Christians, having sat through innumerable Bible studies, sermons, and prayer meetings. We might have memorized verses, fasted, and worshiped for years. But it's often not until seasons of suffering—real pain and difficulty—enter our lives that our faith becomes something more than classroom discussions. It's during those times when the questions about the nature of God and good and evil become particularly poignant.

Though we might consider ourselves to be rock solid in our faith, there are times when, in light of the hurricane or tornado, the job loss or the cancer, we have to wonder, *Where is God? Is He even real? Why is this happening? Why doesn't He do something about it?*

We aren't the first people to ask those questions. Indeed, the question of suffering is one of the most fundamental questions of who God is and how He relates to us.

For me, these questions became particularly meaningful several years ago when I sat in a pediatrician's office and heard that my two-year-old son had leukemia. I found myself asking the fundamental questions of life, as if for the first time, but now processed not through a textbook or a lecture but in the classroom of life. No longer were these merely theoretical issues to be dissected but instead intensely personal issues about God, sin, and the world. In short, I was struggling to see how two truths of Scripture fit together in light of suffering.

God is all-powerful. God is loving. Scripture presents both of these truths in tandem, and yet they seem to contradict each other in light of the problem of pain. Either God, in His love, wants to prevent suffering but is not powerful enough to do so or else He is powerful enough to do so but does not love us enough to intervene. This chapter will show how God's love and power are not at odds and that suffering has great meaning in the life of the Christian.

Not "If" but "When" (Jas. 1:2-4)

As much as we might try, real suffering is not something we can be prepared for. It comes on us like a tidal wave—emotionally, spiritually, and often physically. Perhaps that's one of the reasons why we have so many questions when it happens. We assume that everything is going to be the same tomorrow as it was today, and then BAM! We are hit with something we never saw coming.

It's the violence of the impact that brings these questions and issues to light. But as James tells us, suffering is not the exception for humanity; it's the rule. Digging into the truth that suffering is not a question of "if" but "when" helps us begin to get at the reconciliation between the goodness and the power of God.

2 Consider it a great joy, my brothers, whenever you experience various trials, 3 knowing that the testing of your faith produces endurance. 4 But endurance must do its complete work, so that you may be mature and complete, lacking nothing.

The key word in this passage from James that points us to the inevitability of suffering is "whenever." For James, the issue of suffering was not a question of *if* but instead a question of *when*. I don't know about you, but that doesn't create a sense of confidence in me. It is, nevertheless, a realistic picture of the world in which we live. Here's why. The world is absolutely broken by sin.

Think back to the very beginning. God created a world that was absolutely perfect. In His own estimation, it was "very good." His original creation was marked by absolute harmony. Perhaps you remember the next phase in the story too—a snake. A piece of fruit. And a choice. It was a choice that first sent the shock waves of suffering reverberating through the universe. This is when sin entered the world.

Now we tend to think about sin as doing something bad. Making a wrong choice. Missing the mark. It certainly is those things, but sin goes far wider and deeper than mere actions. In humanity, sin is not just an action but also a heart bent toward evil. It's the condition that makes us delight in doing wrong instead of doing right.

This condition is why just trying harder is simply not enough for us to return to fellowship with God; we must have a completely new heart. That's why only the gospel can truly answer our deepest needs and desires.

But the effects of sin aren't applied exclusively to humanity. Beyond the scope of humanity, sin is what has plunged creation into decay. Tornadoes, earthquakes, and droughts are just as much an effect of the fall in Genesis 3 as lying, lust, and murder.

If we begin to think of sin in these far-reaching terms, we can begin to see why James could write with such confidence that suffering is inevitable. It is, in a sense, one of the things that link all of humanity together. We all live in a world that has been marred by sin. The effects of that marring show up in our pain and suffering as well as our choices. Wherever we come from, whatever our occupations are, and whatever course our lives take, we all exist in a sinful world. Because we do, we all have experienced its dreadful effects.

Christians are not immune to the terrible effects of sin, and part of the answer to how a good God can allow this kind of suffering is beginning to grasp the true extent of the brokenness of the world.

Ultimately, then, though our pain might cause us to ask difficult questions of God, it should also cause us to recognize the gravity and extensiveness of sin. Not that God is punishing us for particular trespasses, but our entire existence must be viewed as broken and in great need of rescue.

That, however, is not the only lens through which we must view our pain. We must also see it through the lens of the gospel. God has settled once and for all the question of His love. If we want to know how much God loves us, we cannot look to our circumstances; we must instead look to the cross.

Think about it in terms of a doorway to a house. You approach a house and immediately go to the door. You might stand at the door for a moment; you might appreciate the craftsmanship of the door; you might even put your hand on it to feel the grain of the wood. But then you knock on the door and enter through it. The door is only the entrance point to the rest of the house.

Suffering can be like that. Suffering brings us to the point of asking the questions of God, but it's only the doorway. The suffering itself does not hold the answers; it's only the entrance point. The answers lie beyond the door, and having walked through it, we find the cross of Jesus Christ waiting on the other side.

The cross is what endures. It's what is substantial. It's what is eternal. That's where we look for the deepest answers to the questions about God's love and power.

James recognized that during times of pain, we would likely ask questions. Big questions. Hard questions. That's why, along with those questions, we must also ask for wisdom (1:5-8). When we do, we can begin to see that suffering for the Christian is not merely a quest for answers; it's a doorway into something much, much deeper.

Not "Why" but "Who" (Job 1:20-22)

After our son was diagnosed with cancer, many of my questions began with the word "Why." I spent many late nights in hospital rooms, rocking a hurting two-year-old boy to sleep, repeating that word over and over again in my mind. But over time, I've come to believe that *why* is often the wrong question during seasons of suffering. I believe this not because I have had some revelation about my son's cancer. Quite the contrary! I don't think we'll ever know the specifics of the *why* this side of heaven.

The reason "Why?" is the wrong question is because that's not really what we're wondering. What we are really wondering is "Who?"

Take the story of Job, for example. Job was a rich man, an upstanding citizen of his community. He had a large family and everything he needed and yet never took any of it for granted. He was continually on his knees before God, even going so far as regularly offering sacrifices on behalf of his children, just in case they had sinned. This was the pattern of life he settled into, but unbeknownst to him, there was a cosmic conversation going on with him at the center.

At God's permission, Satan systematically took apart Job's life, starting with his children. Then his property. Then his physical health. Job was eventually left poor, alone, and sick in emotional, physical, and spiritual pain. But why?

Job didn't have the luxury of reading about his story on the pages of a book. He was living the awful reality. But rather than denying his questions, as we might be tempted to do, he pressed hard into them.

Now, we know from the context of the first two chapters that it was Satan who actually did the afflicting of Job. And yet look at how Job responded:

20 *Then Job stood up, tore his robe, and shaved his head. He fell to the ground and worshiped,* 21 *saying:*
Naked I came from my mother's womb,
and naked I will leave this life.
The LORD gives, and the LORD takes away.
Praise the name of Yahweh.
22 *Throughout all this Job did not sin or blame God for anything.*

When Job wanted to press into rather than deny his circumstances, he turned his attention to God. If God were not okay with the spotlight being shined on Him, then we certainly would not have the explicit statements made in 1:22 and 2:10 reminding us that Job did not sin when he looked at God. The conclusion, then, is that our struggle ultimately is with God.

It's easier in moments of pain to direct your sorrow, disappointment, and anger at Satan or a broken world or random occurrence. It's true that all these are factors, but it can't stop there. If we allow it to, we are robbing God of His power and control and cheating ourselves out of fully processing the magnitude of who He is.

Some would argue that God causes hardship. Others would say He simply fails to prevent tragedies from occurring. Pragmatically, though, the result is the same—we suffer, and whether God acts or doesn't act, He's still at the bottom of it. That means our true conflict is with God.

If we really want to start down the road of asking why, let's not sell ourselves short of following it all the way to the end. At the end, there's God. He's the One in control. He's the only being in the universe that is sovereign. He's the beginning and the end of all things, including our laments. And that's probably why we don't want to follow the trail all the way to the end, because if God is at the end, then we aren't just asking why about our circumstances.

We are asking about the foundations of what we think—what we hope—is true. We are asking about the nature of good and evil. We are wondering about the validity of the love of God. We are pondering the extent of His compassion and wisdom.

Job 31:40 sums up the end of Job's search like this: "The words of Job are concluded." What else was there left to say? Job had clung to the notion that he wanted an explanation from God despite the accusations from his supposed friends. He had the courage and perseverance to keep on asking, to keep insisting, to keep pressing into the depths of his despair. He refused to stop short on his search, and that search led him into the throne room of heaven. Then something amazing, and perhaps terrifying, happened—God started talking back.

God answered Job from a whirlwind, a manifestation of God's power. Though Job may have been upright, he was calling the wisdom and appropriateness of God's choices into question. It all added up to a simple question that, for the life of him, Job couldn't answer on his own—*Why?* Here's the troubling thing, at least at first glance: In the next four chapters, God spoke to Job. He pointed to every imaginable element of nature, describing His power as He directed everything from the swimming patterns of giant fish to the fall of rain. But nowhere in this diatribe did God ever tell Job the answer to his question.

After 37 chapters of accusations, questions, and pain, the answer God gave was not the *why* Job was looking for. It was the *Who* he wasn't.

God did not crack the door of eternity and say, "See, this whole thing started when Satan came walking in here…" He did not take Job into the future to show him the good that would come from his struggle. He did not reveal the way He would redeem Job's pain. He gave not one single answer to Job's specific questions, just descriptions of Himself.

While that may seem unsatisfying on our end, to know that God doesn't offer answers or promise a glimpse "on the inside," we've got to ask ourselves the question "Would knowing why really help?"

I had always thought that the question of *why* would be very important to me when tragedy and suffering struck. Surprisingly, though, I didn't care much about the *why* behind Joshua's cancer. *Why* doesn't bring back the lost time. *Why* doesn't gather up the tears we've shed. *Why* doesn't make the ache go away. *Why* doesn't help with the anxiety of the future. But *Who* does.

God is the Redeemer of moments both small and large. God gathers up our tears and holds them in His hands. God is the Healer of the soul and the Caretaker of the future. *Who* helps tremendously in ways that *why* never could.

The truth is, what people in pain need, more than answers, is God. And when we are willing to push deeply into pain and the questions that come with it, we don't necessarily find all the answers—but we find God. He's at the core of our questions. And He Himself is the answer to our pain.

Not "Me" but "Us" (2 Cor. 1:3-7)

One of the most difficult parts about walking through a season of suffering is the intense feeling of loneliness. You begin to resent statements such as "I know how you feel" because the truth is no one really does. They can certainly sympathize with you, but only you know the depth of your struggle. Consequently, you really are alone. And yet…

And yet Jesus is no stranger to suffering. He is personally familiar with all our experiences. When no one else knows how we feel, Jesus does. When we choose to engage these questions and then find God Himself waiting at the end of them, we also find the comfort of a knowing and understanding Jesus. But that comfort isn't meant for us only.

One of the ends, one of the results, of our search for that place where the goodness and power of God meet is the understanding that God wants to comfort us so that we might be a comfort to other people. In Paul's mind, one of the reasons he suffered so greatly was specifically so that he might be a comfort to the Christians in the church in Corinth.

3 Praise the God and Father of our Lord Jesus Christ, the Father of mercies and the God of all comfort. 4 He comforts us in all our affliction, so that we may be able to comfort those who are in any kind of affliction, through the comfort we ourselves receive from God. 5 For as the sufferings of Christ overflow to us, so through Christ our comfort also overflows. 6 If we are afflicted, it is for your comfort and salvation. If we are comforted, it is for your comfort, which is experienced in your endurance of the same sufferings that we suffer. 7 And our hope for you is firm, because we know that as you share in the sufferings, so you will share in the comfort.

Through our suffering, God bonds us together in the church. We serve as tangible expressions of the deep and abiding love and care of Jesus Christ to each other. This is especially important for us because, no matter how rock solid our faith might seem to be, we are incredibly forgetful people. Think about it in terms of our suffering.

We know God is loving. We know this not only because the Bible tells us it's true but because we believe that the love of God is demonstrated in the cross of Jesus Christ. We also know that God is wise. Though we might not understand the reasons behind our suffering, we know they are there. We further know that God is powerful and faithful and a host of other things. But there's nothing like a diagnosis, an end to a relationship, a job loss, or some other jarring life transition to make us temporarily forget those things.

So how are we reminded of what we know to be true? We read the Scriptures. We sing. We pray. But there's something else. We are reminded when someone—someone who has suffered in like fashion—steps alongside us and gently helps us remember the comforting words of Jesus.

Conclusion

Easy answers are not satisfying to those who are dealing with intense suffering. Unfortunately, Christians have an immense propensity to use comforting words like a blunt instrument. Sometimes the best reminder isn't that your child is in heaven, or that all things are working together for good, or that God is going to set everything right, even though all those things are wonderfully true. Sometimes the best reminder is tears from one grieving alongside you.

The church, then, is the string around its own finger. We demonstrate the proven love of God when we weep with those who weep and rejoice with those who rejoice. Along the way, we continue to trust in a God whose reasons for permitting suffering go beyond our finite limitations but ultimately point us to the cross of Christ.

HYMN OF *Response*

Be Thou my Vision, O Lord of my heart;
Naught be all else to me, save that Thou art:
Thou my best thought, by day or by night,
Waking or sleeping, Thy presence my light.

High King of heaven, my victory won,
May I reach heaven's joys, O bright heav'n's Sun!
Heart of my own heart, whatever befall,
Still be my Vision, O Ruler of all.

Devotions

God's Promises

When we say that God always keeps His promises, we typically think of the kind of promises that lead to our comfort. So yes, in that instance, we do indeed want to claim the promises of God. Like kids who have been promised a treat after dinner, we sit at the table of the Father counting on Him to keep His word.

But these aren't the only promises of God. And not all of God's promises are so easy to claim: "You will have suffering in this world" (John 16:33). It's not a "maybe, maybe not" kind of thing. It's a promise, as real as God's constant presence, as His engineering of circumstances for our good, and as His abiding love. It's a promise.

The promises of God aren't like a cafeteria line where you can take the ones that taste like jello and leave the ones that taste like broccoli. It's a full plate that comes to you in Christ, like it or not. God always keeps His promises—you will have trouble. But amazingly, even in this promise, the gospel echoes on, for that's not the only thing Jesus promised in this passage. After this promise of suffering and trial, Jesus plainly said that despite this, we should be courageous because "I have conquered the world."

That's the good news that accompanies the not-so-comfortable promises of God. Though we will have trouble, though we will suffer, though we might even be brought before rulers, governments, and authorities to answer for our faith, Jesus has conquered the world. We can, then, have very clear expectations from God because He keeps these promises. Will there be difficulty? Yes. Will He be present with us? Yes. Will His victory be declared over all creation? Absolutely. God always keeps His promises.

Pause and Reflect

1   Do you claim some promises of God and not others?

- -

2   How can you have a more balanced understanding of God's promises?

Questioning God's Love

Jesus loves me, this I know, for the Bible tells me so. Right?

Very true. But there are those moments when the love of God is drawn into question, and most of the time, those moments coincide with times of suffering. I know that my wife loves me. I know that my kids love me (most of the time). And I know that my parents love me. How?

Part of it is because of their words. They tell me they love me. But it's more than that. I know—really know—they love me because they show me.

It's interesting, then, that when Paul reflected on the love of God, he used some very specific language: "For while we were still helpless, at the appointed moment, Christ died for the ungodly. For rarely will someone die for a just person—though for a good person perhaps someone might even dare to die. But God proves His own love for us in that while we were still sinners, Christ died for us!" (Rom. 5:6-8).

See it? God proves. He demonstrates. He backs up His claim. He closes the case. He settles the issue. He leaves no doubt.

How do we know God loves us? We know He loves us because of the cross. That's how we know. It sounds so simple, but if you find yourself in a situation in which you question the love of God because of your circumstances, think of the cross. Think of Jesus, over and over again. The Father did not spare the Son but gave Him up for you. And for me. Because He loves us. Case closed.

Pause and Reflect

1   How can you remind yourself to think deeply about the cross today?

----

2   How might doing so change the way you approach difficult circumstances in life?

SOMETIMES "NOTHING" IS THE BEST THING

The friends of Job got it right at first. They went to their friend offering their presence. For seven days, they sat. That was the best thing they could do. But then they messed everything up by opening their mouths.

Sometimes, for those in grief, *nothing* is the best thing you can say. We have, as Christians, an amazing propensity to say dumb things to those in pain. The things we say might be theologically accurate (or not, see Job's friends). Regardless, just because they're *right* doesn't mean they're *helpful*. Not in that moment.

But still we feel the need to say that everything will be okay, that all will work together for good, that he's in a better place now. All true, and yet none offer the balm of healing that lessens the pain. I wonder what our motivation might be. Do we want to offer a word of hope? A consolation of truth? Or are we so uncomfortable with deep, gut-wrenching pain that we are actually trying to make *ourselves* feel better so that we don't have to sit in the middle of that muck and mire? Of course, there is a time to point the grieving back to the words God has given us for comfort. However, that truth must be wielded carefully and thoughtfully, lest we bring a theological sledgehammer down onto the heads of the grieving.

Jesus knew better than us that sometimes the best thing you can say is actually nothing. So in John 11, when He met with Lazarus' sister Mary in her grief, He offered no theological treatise, no simple explanation for death, not even a statement of His own actions that had allowed the death. There would be another time for that. But not right then. Right then, in His great compassion and wisdom, Jesus offered something equally right and yet infinitely more helpful—Jesus wept.

Pause and Reflect

1   Why is it meaningful to you that Jesus wept rather than offered an explanation for suffering?

----

2   How specifically might you follow in the example of Jesus?

Discussion Questions

1 When have you asked questions about the trials in your life? Do you think it's wrong for a Christian to ask these kinds of questions? Why or why not?

2 Do you have the tendency to turn inward and remain isolated during times of difficulty? Why or why not?

3 Think back to a season of suffering in your own life. Did God use that suffering to lead you into a different kind of relationship with Him? How so? Why might suffering be an effective means of spiritual growth, as James described?

4 Based on Job 1:20-22, how would you describe Job? How did he respond to his suffering? Why do you think the Bible explicitly points out that Job did not sin in what he said?

5 Read Job 38:1-11. What emotion do you imagine God's voice conveyed? What was the basic message of God's answer to Job?

6 Why do you think God never answered Job's question of *why*? Have you ever heard an answer to your own question of *why*?

7 Do you think knowing all the reasons for your pain would help? If so, why? If not, why not?

8 Read Job 42:1-6. How did Job respond to God's revelation? What do you think he thought about his experience in looking back on it? Why might a greater understanding of the power and character of God be what all of us in pain really need?

9 Think about your own experience. Were you comforted by someone who had received the comfort of Jesus? How so? Have you been able to comfort someone else through the comfort you received from God? How?

10 Why is it important to pray for wisdom as you seek to comfort those in pain? What are some examples from Scripture of Jesus comforting those in pain? What can we learn from His example?

Chapter 9

By J. D. Greear

Hell

Is Hell Real and Necessary?

Voices from *the Church*

"I am conscious of the fact that the subject of hell is not a very pleasant one. It is very unpopular, controversial, and misunderstood...As a minister I must deal with it. I cannot ignore it." [1]
–Billy Graham

Voices from *Church History*

"There are only two kinds of people in the end: those who say to God, 'Thy will be done,' and those to whom God says in the end, '*Thy* will be done.'" [2]
–C. S. Lewis (1898-1963)

Big questions. They don't go away at the moment you become a Christian. You may approach them differently, with a faith that seeks understanding and a willing submission to the authority of God's Word, but the questions are still there. And hell is a big one.

Some people hear Christian teaching about a place called hell and they immediately reject everything else too. "Well, if Christians believe that, then Christianity can't possibly be true! How could anyone take Christianity seriously if there is a place called hell where God sends people who reject Him?" And so, many people recoil from an image of God that seems cruel, mean, and vengeful, as if He were a sadist who delights in torturing people for not believing in Him.

Then there's the question of fairness. Doesn't the punishment exceed the crime? You live a normal life, 70 or 80 years. You're not perfect, but you're not all that bad. And then you go to hell for all eternity? Eternal punishment for 70 years of misdemeanors?

The doctrine of hell is personal for me. It nearly destroyed and then saved my faith. At first, I could not understand how a loving God and an eternal place like hell could coexist. In college, the tension almost wrecked my faith.

But later, it was the doctrine of hell that caused me to reckon with the majesty of God. Hell led me to embrace everything else the Bible says about God's nature and rule—things I could not fully understand. The severity of hell showed me the heinousness of my sin.

Eventually, I came to realize that if God is as big and holy as the Bible says He is, then I'm foolish for thinking He should fit into my simple categories. Until you concede the existence of a God far beyond your comprehension, you'll be baffled by your inability to figure everything out and angered that He doesn't operate the way you think He ought to. The reality of eternal justice helps us see just how big God is, and this in turn puts us in the proper posture to believe.

In this chapter, we are going to look at the why behind the reality of hell. Because the Scriptures are clear that hell is a real place, we will not spend our time proving its existence. Instead, we will examine the Scriptures to understand why it exists. In the end, we will see how the reality of hell honors the choices of God's image bearers and how eternal justice magnifies the glory and holiness of God. Then we will see how the reality of hell ought to fuel our passion to see lost people come to know Christ and be saved.

The reality of hell honors the choices of God's image bearers (Luke 16:19-31).

Sometimes Christians try to avoid the subject of hell by pitting the Old and New Testaments against each other. Hell? Oh, that's God: Version 1.0, God in His junior high years when He was cranky! You've got to remember that Jesus was meek and mild, all about love and compassion. Of course, a cursory reading of the Gospels blows up that myth. Jesus talked more about hell than heaven. As an example, let's look at one of the stories Jesus told—"The Rich Man and Lazarus."

19 *"There was a rich man who would dress in purple and fine linen, feasting lavishly every day.* 20 *But a poor man named Lazarus, covered with sores, was left at his gate.* 21 *He longed to be filled with what fell from the rich man's table, but instead the dogs would come and lick his sores.* 22 *One day the poor man died and was carried away by the angels to Abraham's side. The rich man also died and was buried.* 23 *And being in torment in Hades, he looked up and saw Abraham a long way off, with Lazarus at his side.* 24 *'Father Abraham!' he called out, 'Have mercy on me and send Lazarus to dip the tip of his finger in water and cool my tongue, because I am in agony in this flame!'*

25 *"'Son,' Abraham said, 'remember that during your life you received your good things, just as Lazarus received bad things, but now he is comforted here, while you are in agony.* 26 *Besides all this, a great chasm has been fixed between us and you, so that those who want to pass over from here to you cannot; neither can those from there cross over to us.'*

27 *"'Father,' he said, 'then I beg you to send him to my father's house—* 28 *because I have five brothers—to warn them, so they won't also come to this place of torment.'*

29 *"But Abraham said, 'They have Moses and the prophets; they should listen to them.'*

30 *"'No, father Abraham,' he said. 'But if someone from the dead goes to them, they will repent.'*

31 *"But he told him, 'If they don't listen to Moses and the prophets, they will not be persuaded if someone rises from the dead.'"*

The story of the rich man and Lazarus tells us several things about what eternal judgment looks like. But a key truth we see in this account is how the rich man's choices during life are ratified after his death.

Take a closer look at the rich man. The first thing we notice is how successful he was. Interesting how Jesus tells us the poor man's name ("Lazarus") but only describes the rich man by his riches. Apparently, the basis of this man's identity was his wealth.

We see in this man's pursuit of riches a microcosm of what all sin is—idolatry. One aspect of sin is the choice to draw ultimate fulfillment from something other than God. For many people, it's being liked, being respected and admired in your career, having a good marriage or well-behaved kids. Whatever it is you simply must have in order to be happy and fulfilled is a false god. It's what defines you and your pursuits. For this man, it was money.

The rich man's love of money didn't keep him from being religious. Not at all. In his agony, he called out to father Abraham. This was the kind of man who probably lived a moral life as a decent citizen. He wasn't opposed to God at the level of belief. But it becomes painfully clear that the rich man did not know God. You see, sometimes our religious activities (even as Christians) aren't born out of genuine love for God but are intended to increase our social position, to earn a place in heaven, or to carry on traditions. That's why, in the midst of his suffering, this man didn't call on God. He asked for Abraham. He knew his religion, but he didn't know God.

The strongest piece of evidence that this man didn't know God was his lack of concern for the poor. Those who know and love God are radically generous with finances. It's when we think we've earned our salvation that we don't have compassion on those in need. But when we realize all we have is a gift, it makes us compassionate. On earth, this rich man was unmoved by the needs of others; he turned a deaf ear to Lazarus. (Even in hell, he still views Lazarus as his water boy!) Though he was extremely religious, he had not had an encounter with the grace of God.

So what do we have here? A man who looks great on the outside, while inside, his core is rotting. He is defined by his idols. He doesn't know or love God. He worships money and lives for himself.

At the end of his life, the rich man gets what he wanted—life without God. But life without God wasn't what he expected. It is hell. The man's rejection of God in this life continued into the next. But instead of enjoying life without God, he experienced eternal torment. Interesting, isn't it? Before we see the man in hell, we see the evidence of hell in the man.

Life with God was God's original intention for all humanity; life without Him is death. Like being a fish out of water, dying endlessly in the hot sun, a human being who rejects God is shut off from eternal joy.

There are two common descriptions the Bible gives for hell: fire and darkness. Fire indicates insatiable desire. Fire consumes things but is never satisfied. Leave a fire unchecked, and it grows and grows. It is never full. The rich man's life was like that—never satisfied, always consuming things, abusing other people. Before the consuming fires of hell reached the man, the man burned with consuming fire for his idols.

Hell is the culmination of telling God to "get out." That's why hell is described as darkness. God is light; His absence is darkness. Right now on earth, we experience light, things like love, friendship, the beauty of creation—remnants of the light of God's presence. These earthly enjoyments are akin to the light of the sun's rays; they emanate from God. They warm us, but their ultimate source is God. And when you shut off God, ultimately you'll lose them.

Take sunlight, for example. If the sun were extinguished, it would take eight minutes before its rays would disappear from earth. In God's grace, we live in a world with the light of God still present. But when you tell God you don't want Him as Lord, eventually you get your wish. But without God, you lose all of His gifts. That's why the rich man in this story is in torment. He got what we wanted (life without God) but not what he expected (satisfaction).

When people hear about hell, they object to it, thinking that it means God doesn't love us. But the Bible is clear that God takes no pleasure in the death of the wicked (Ezek. 18:23). He desires that all would come to repentance (2 Pet. 3:9). His love for us is most manifestly demonstrated in the cross of Jesus Christ. Even in this story, Abraham calls the rich man with a tender name ("son").

But why even make hell? Why create a place for humans to suffer? The biblical answer is He didn't. Jesus asserted that hell was made for the Evil One and the angels who joined his rebellion (Matt. 25:41). It was not created for humanity. But in honoring the choices of the humans who bear His image, God sends to hell those who refuse to bow the knee to His lordship. There are two options: life with God or life without Him. Rejecting God is choosing hell.

The reality of hell magnifies the glory of God (Ex. 9:13-17).

13 *Then the* LORD *said to Moses, "Get up early in the morning and present yourself to Pharaoh. Tell him: This is what Yahweh, the God of the Hebrews says: Let My people go, so that they may worship Me.* 14 *Otherwise, I am going to send all My plagues against you, your officials, and your people. Then you will know there is no one like Me in all the earth.* 15 *By now I could have stretched out My hand and struck you and your people with a plague, and you would have been obliterated from the earth.* 16 *However, I have let you live for this purpose: to show you My power and to make My name known in all the earth.* 17 *You are still acting arrogantly against My people by not letting them go.*

God is going to get glory. Either He is going to receive glory by the willing submission of those who repent of their sin and trust in His Son or He is going to receive glory through the manifestation of His righteous judgment against those who spurn Him. Either way, He will be glorified.

This passage in Exodus is a great example of how salvation and judgment go hand in hand. God's glorious love was manifested in the way He rescued the Israelites from bondage to Egyptian oppressors. At the same time, God's glorious justice was manifested in the way He sent plagues upon the wicked. The salvation of God's people took place through the judgment of those who had set themselves against Him.

When God shows mercy, He is glorious. When God executes justice, He is glorious. Come to grips with the magnificence of God and some of the "big questions" related to Christianity disappear.

Think about how great is God's power compared to ours. He spoke the worlds into existence. He created the nebulae and the planets and the stars and the complexities of the atom and the molecule with just a word! One strand of DNA can store enough information to fill up 1,000 sets of the *Encyclopaedia Britannica*,[3] while you have problems getting your DVD player to work right with your cable box!

Now, if there is a God, then His wisdom is also infinite. By extension, His wisdom is as high above yours as His power is above yours. So shouldn't you realize there will necessarily be aspects of God that may not make sense to you?

One of the reasons I think people in our secular culture have trouble believing in God is because we talk about Him with so little sense of wonder and awe at his majesty. Charles Misner, one of Einstein's students, wrote about the famous scientist's lack of interest in religion: "[The design of the universe is] very magnificent and should not be taken for granted. In fact, I believe that is why Einstein had so little use for organized religion, although he strikes me as a basically very religious man. He must have looked at what the preachers said about God and felt that they were blaspheming. He had seen much more majesty than they had ever imagined, and they were just not talking about the real thing. My guess is that he simply felt that religions he'd run across did not have proper respect...for the author of the Universe."[4]

Some of you may be thinking, *I understand why hell exists and why it's necessary that people who reject God must go there. But why these images of fire? It makes it seem like God is angry at sin!* Good point. And you're right. God is angry at sin. The Bible is clear that God is wrathful toward sin.

But this wrath is not divorced from God's love. No. It's because you love someone that you are rightly angered when you see something that is opposed to them. It's God's love for His creation that leads Him to be rightfully angry when He sees people destroying one another, committing atrocious acts of violence and injustice, hurting and abusing themselves and the world around them.

God's anger is a righteous anger. The greatest and most egregious injustice in the universe was our refusal to live for and give glory to God. Don't compare yourselves to Hitler and the "really bad people." Start comparing yourselves to Jesus, the perfect righteous One, the One who shows us how God originally intended all human beings to be.

God's anger is personal because His love is personal. A woman who discovers her husband is committing adultery gets angry. Why? Out of love. A shrug of the shoulders would communicate a lack of love. It's the anger that demonstrates the ferocity of exclusive love.

The Bible often describes our sin as adultery. Our decision to live without God and to spurn His advances toward us is cosmic adultery. Even our good deeds on earth are done in the context of a life of unspeakable injustice in not loving God with all of our hearts.

That's why hell is infinite, never ending. People say it's not fair that finite sin would receive infinite punishment. But don't forget, our sin was against an infinite God, and justice requires an infinite punishment. Hell is a very clear statement to us about the greatness and majesty of God. Hell is what it is because God is who God is.

Some people think they're doing God a favor by *lessening* hell, but what they're doing is diminishing the greatness of God. The truth is we think hell is severe because we don't think trampling on the glory of God is that big of a deal. We think the big deal in the universe is us. I know this is horribly offensive to us as humans who think the universe is all about us—but it's not. This whole creation is a theater to the only true, good, all-powerful God. He is the big deal in the universe, and everything works to His glory. Hell itself is a permanent monument to the greatness of His name.

But no matter how great and mighty God is, He is also loving. That's why He invites us to know and love Him, to enjoy Him and share in His delight. God is so loving that He even sacrificed His own Son for us so that even after we trampled His glory, He could allow us to know and enjoy Him again.

The reality of hell gives urgency to evangelism (Rom. 10:11-17).

The reality of hell shows us the extent of God's love in saving us. Though some people see hell as a blemish on God's love, the Bible presents the opposite. Hell magnifies for us the love of God in showing how far God went—how much He went through—to save us.

We sing, "I'll never know how much it cost to see my sin upon the cross." One of the ways you understand how much God loves us is seeing what it cost Him to save us. That's why Jesus spoke more about hell than anyone else in the Bible. Because He wanted us to see what He was going to endure on the cross on our behalf.

The reason many Christians don't want to believe God would send people to hell is because they don't think they are worthy of hell. Almost all of our apologetic difficulties go back to assuming our goodness and God's smallness.

But when we see that we deserve hell, we see how glorious the cross is, which was the clearest picture of God's majestic greatness and love reaching down to the depths of our wickedness. You can't really appreciate the cross until you embrace hell. The reason most Christians don't weep at the cross is they don't embrace, or really understand, the doctrine of hell. Hell is what leads you to worship, to stand in awe of the grace of the cross.

Now what are we supposed to do once we stand in awe of the cross? Start running to others with the news. The apostle Paul wrote:

11 *Now the Scripture says, Everyone who believes on Him will not be put to shame,* 12 *for there is no distinction between Jew and Greek, since the same Lord of all is rich to all who call on Him.* 13 *For everyone who calls on the name of the Lord will be saved.*

14 *But how can they call on Him they have not believed in? And how can they believe without hearing about Him? And how can they hear without a preacher?* 15 *And how can they preach unless they are sent? As it is written: How beautiful are the feet of those who announce the gospel of good things!* 16 *But all did not obey the gospel. For Isaiah says, Lord, who has believed our message?* 17 *So faith comes from what is heard, and what is heard comes through the message about Christ.*

Conclusion

The reality of hell presents us with an option. We either deny the Bible's teaching on this subject or we ignore it, choosing to affirm it in our doctrinal statements but living functionally as if it weren't really there.

Or there's one more option. We can be filled with the missionary zeal described in Romans 10—to take the gospel to those who don't know Christ.

Think back to the story of the rich man and Lazarus. Remember how the rich man wanted to send someone back from the dead to warn his brothers? Hell made an evangelist out of the rich man. What about us?

Devotions

Untouchable Holiness

In Exodus 19, God instructed the leaders of Israel to set up a perimeter around Mount Sinai. If anyone crossed over that line, even accidentally, they would be immediately struck dead. This applied to the rulers, the priests, the parents, the children, and even household pets. God told Moses why a few chapters later—"Because you cannot look at My face and live."

God is a God of such infinite perfection that even the slightest sin in His presence leads to immediate annihilation. When Isaiah, the prophet of God, saw God upon His throne, he fell upon his face, terrified and sure that he was about to die. When Uzzah reached out his hand to steady the ark of the covenant, God struck him dead…because he assumed his hand was less dirty than the ground.

God is a God whose holiness and perfection is so complete that God told them that if a sinner sees Him, he or she would die. People speak glibly about "seeing God." If God ripped the roof off this place and you and I looked up into His face, we'd immediately die.

The doctrine of God's holiness is connected to the doctrine of hell. I know that hell has fallen greatly out of favor today, but hell is what hell is because the holiness of God is what it is. Hell is not one degree hotter than our sin demands that it be. Hell should make our mouths stand agape at the righteousness, justice, and holiness of God.

Pause and Reflect

1   Are you willing to pay a social price for standing apart from the world when it comes to your views on hell?

---

2   How does the reality of God's holiness convict us of sin and cause us to run to Christ for forgiveness?

PERSONAL PREFERENCE

The reason many people today have difficulty with the idea of *hell* is because society has relegated religion to the realm of personal preference. In other words, religions may be helpful, but we ought not consider one true and another false. We judge religions in terms of how beneficial we find them, not by whether or not they are true.

For many, religions are like Pepsi and Coke. Who's to say which is better? It depends on your taste, right?

But the apostles didn't preach religion. They preached the resurrection. They focused on the resurrection of Jesus Christ as the central moment in history. Consider the sermons in the Book of Acts. We don't see the apostles asking questions such as "Are you benefiting from your religion? Why not try ours?" Instead, they proclaimed the resurrection.

If Jesus really rose from the dead, then we are no longer talking about personal preferences. What you do with Jesus is of crucial importance.

No longer are we talking about religion in terms of personal preference. Now, we're talking about religion in terms of personal power. If we believe Jesus came out of the grave on Easter morning, then we must accept whatever He says about heaven, hell, and the nature of salvation. We can't say, "That's not to my liking," or, "That's not my taste." The question now is "What is the truth?"

Pause and Reflect

1   In what ways are you tempted to make your religious belief merely a matter of preference and not objective truth?

----

2   How is one's view of eternity affected by the reality of the resurrection?

THE URGENT MISSION

It's one thing to affirm the reality of hell in our heads, but it's another thing entirely to be gripped by this truth to the point it affects our actions. If we truly believe that people who do not know Christ will face eternity without Him in judgment, then certain implications follow. Right now, one third of the people on our planet claim to be Christians. Two thirds do not name the name of Jesus. Some estimate that there are 3 billion people who have little to no access to the gospel. There are more than six thousand Unreached People Groups.

As Christians, it is not enough for us to check off the box "Hell" on our list of doctrines. This truth is meant to change our lives. It's meant to give our mission a sense of urgency. God doesn't expect us to speculate endlessly about the fate of the unevangelized or the nature of hell. He expects us to believe what He has said and to get busy telling others about Jesus.

When it comes to missions, many people pray like this, "God, if you tell me to go, I'll go." Instead, considering the urgency of our mission, we ought to pray this way: "Here I am, Lord. Send me. Use my life as a seed to bring great harvest." You don't have to go overseas to be a missionary. You can be a missionary in your community. You can support those who do go to the hard places where people have never heard the gospel.

Your life will look different than mine. The Holy Spirit will use you in ways unique to your gifts and situation. But make no mistake. He will use you if you are surrendered to His plan and purposes. Don't deny the doctrine of hell, ignore it, or downplay it. Affirm the truth, and then surrender to God's global mission

Pause and Reflect

1   What are you doing to help get the gospel to people who have never heard the name of Jesus?

- -

2   What is your responsibility to share the gospel with the people in your own community?

DISCUSSION QUESTIONS

1 Why is the idea that God would punish people in hell so offensive to people today? Do you wrestle with this teaching? What are some of your own doubts and concerns?

2 What are some differences you notice between Lazarus and the rich man in Luke 16:19-31?

3 Would you think of the rich man as a bad man? Why or why not? What are some false gods worshiped by religious people? How does our understanding of idolatry during life connect with the idea of eternal suffering after death?

4 What biblical images come to mind when you think about hell? What do these images communicate about hell?

5 How is the Bible's portrait of God different from the image many in our society have? How does the vision of His majesty and love differ from the sentimental view of love prevalent in our culture?

6 What is the connection between understanding the severity of God's judgment and the extravagance of His grace? How does a biblical understanding of hell increase our view of God?

7 In what ways does the gap between God's infinite knowledge and our finite understanding encourage you when you don't fully grasp His ways?

8 Sometimes people will say, "God looks at your heart," as a way of avoiding difficult truths about eternal judgment. Considering what the Bible says about the human heart, why should this truth cause us to recognize our sin instead of our sincerity?

9 Do you think pastors and leaders talk too much or too little about judgment today?

10 In what ways should the reality of hell increase our sense of urgency in reaching the lost? How does the reality of hell impact our understanding of our mission as Christ's followers?

Part 3

THE BIG DEBATES

Because of sin, humanity rejects God's good plan and purpose for His creation. We see the effects of this in the big debates of our time, debates over sex, marriage, the sacredness of human life, and the proper concern for others and our world. A God-centered worldview provides the proper perspective, not so we can win an argument but so we can faithfully display the glory of God in the world.

Chapter 10

By Matt Chandler

Holy Sexuality

Sexuality as God's Good Gift

VOICES FROM *Church History*

"We must exhibit simultaneously the holiness of God and the love of God. Anything else than this simultaneous exhibition presents a caricature of our God to the world rather than showing Him forth." [1]
–Francis Schaeffer (1912-1984)

VOICES FROM *the Church*

"Our struggles and temptations often trigger sin, but they never cause it. The root cause is always the heart and its sinful desires." [2]
–Tim Chester

As Christians, we've always been oddballs when it comes to our views on sexuality. When you take the Christian view of sex and place it in the context of world history and contemporary ideas about human sexuality, you see just how much we stand out. Think about it: no sex before marriage; no sex outside of marriage; no homosexuality; and the list goes on.

The problem is that our culture resists this distinctiveness. The world would have us conform to its pattern of thinking. That's why, when we say we hold to a biblical view of sexuality, we're often labeled as intolerant, repressive, bigoted, etc.

As a result, we've often stayed silent. We've not addressed hot button issues related to sexual morality. Why? Maybe because anytime you take a particular sin and address it, you risk elevating it above all other sins. We don't want to do that here. We need to look at all sin, sexual or otherwise, within the broader context of the Bible's teaching.

So in this session, we're going to look at sexuality in the broader context of all humanity's sexual sinfulness. As we go forward, keep in mind that whenever we are discussing this issue, we're talking about people, not position statements. We are talking about human beings who deserve to be treated with dignity and respect because of the God whose image they bear. And ultimately, we're talking about us—our own sinful hearts that need redemption.

In this chapter, we will look at God's design for human sexuality as described in the Scriptures. As Christians, we need to recognize that sexuality is a gift from God and that His purpose and design for sex is intended to bring us joy. We also need to realize that we are all sexual sinners in need of forgiveness that comes through Jesus Christ. God calls us to respond to sexual sin by repenting of wrong and trusting His Spirit to empower us as we walk in holiness.

Recognize sexuality as given by God for our good (Gen. 2:8-9,15-25).

8 *The* LORD *God planted a garden in Eden, in the east, and there He placed the man He had formed.* 9 *The* LORD *God caused to grow out of the ground every tree pleasing in appearance and good for food, including the tree of life in the middle of the garden, as well as the tree of the knowledge of good and evil.*
....

15 *The* LORD *God took the man and placed him in the garden of Eden to work it and watch over it.* 16 *And the* LORD *God commanded the man, "You are free to eat from any tree of the garden,* 17 *but you must not eat from the tree of the knowledge of good and evil, for on the day you eat from it, you will certainly die."* 18 *Then the* LORD *God said, "It is not good for the man to be alone. I will make a helper as his complement."* 19 *So the* LORD *God formed out of the ground every*

wild animal and every bird of the sky, and brought each to the man to see what he would call it. And whatever the man called a living creature, that was its name. 20 The man gave names to all the livestock, to the birds of the sky, and to every wild animal; but for the man no helper was found as his complement. 21 So the LORD God caused a deep sleep to come over the man, and he slept. God took one of his ribs and closed the flesh at that place. 22 Then the LORD God made the rib He had taken from the man into a woman and brought her to the man. 23 And the man said:

> *This one, at last, is bone of my bone and flesh of my flesh;
> this one will be called "woman," for she was taken from man.*

24 This is why a man leaves his father and mother and bonds with his wife, and they become one flesh. 25 Both the man and his wife were naked, yet felt no shame.

If we're going to follow Jesus' lead in understanding human sexuality, then we have to go where He pointed us. When asked about the purpose for marriage (Matt. 19), Jesus pointed to Genesis 2. Back to the beginning.

Genesis 1–2 shows us how God created everything and called it good. In love, He placed man and woman in the garden of Eden to enjoy what He had created. God gave us good things, not so that we would simply enjoy them for their own sake but so that our hearts would be stirred with gratitude and joyful worship of God, the Giver.

Take food, for example. God gave us food, not so food would become the ultimate source of our joy but so that food would stir up worship and gladness in our hearts toward God. Whenever I am out of the country for a few weeks, I can't wait to get home to eat Tex Mex. It's a worshipful experience for me, really. Chips and hot sauce stir up joy and worship in my heart toward the Creator who gives us such wonderful tastes.

The same is true of other things, such as sex. In fact, everything that exists was intended to roll up into worship and joy in the Creator of all good gifts. It's important to remember this. Otherwise, we might think that God's commands are designed to press us down and squelch our joy. We might think God demands our begrudging submission, as if He were a "meany" in the sky waiting to send a thunderbolt toward anyone having a good time.

Nothing could be further from the truth. When God gives us His commands regarding our actions, He is lining us up with how He created the universe to work. God's law is intended to restore the *shalom*, the peace, of the garden. He doesn't want to rob us of joy but to lead us into its fullness.

If we don't have the right view of God, we'll never have the right view of sexuality. Think about it this way. Let's say you ask me what my marriage is like.

A **GOD-CENTERED** WORLDVIEW

I respond with a frown, "Well, I made a vow! Eleven years ago, I stood in front of God, a preacher, and a bunch of friends. I said I would love her, and that's why I can't leave her. I made a vow." Now, if I were to talk about marriage this way, would you think it's beautiful? Would it make you want to be married? Probably not! It sounds like I'm in a relationship I would rather not have.

But let's say you ask me about my marriage, and I start talking about my wife's outer beauty and her inner beauty. And I sound all corny when I talk about how in love I am. Do you see the difference? When I am joyfully united to my wife, the picture of marriage is glorious. Both examples include a vow, but the second exalts marriage for what it is intended to be.

The same is true regarding sex. When we read this passage in Genesis, we can see how lovely the woman is to the man. We see how gloriously unashamed they are together. This is God's intention—that human beings would enjoy God's gifts by seeing how they reveal the loving heart of God, the Giver.

In the end, God's commands about sex are about lining us up with how He created the universe to work. But even though God's law is for our good, the world resists any attempt to see morality as prescribed by God in this way.

Left on our own, we want morality to be decided by consensus. Whatever most people think, that's the way it goes. It makes sense to think of consensus morality if we humans are the ultimate authority. But the Bible won't let us go there. The Bible reveals God, and because this God speaks, we believe morality isn't something that humans decide. It's something that God reveals.

Realize we are all sexual sinners (Rom. 1:21-28).

The beautiful harmony of Genesis 2 isn't what we experience today, is it? Almost everyone, regardless of religious persuasion, knows that something's gone wrong in the world. If we head to a bookstore, the largest section of books is going to be titled "Self-Help." Why? Because we all know something's wrong. And we also know something's wrong with us. That's why so many go to these books that offer solutions: Let's get your finances straight. Let's work on your abs. Let's work on your emotional state.

All of our problems go back to the scene immediately following the beauty of Genesis 2. Adam and Eve committed treason against God by sinning against Him. The moment they sinned, their relationship with God was broken. Because of God's curse on sin, the universe began to fracture. The *shalom* of the garden was disrupted. The rhythm of the universe went out of sync. Everything is off.

Why is the universe such a mess? In Romans 1, the apostle Paul unpacked the foundational sin that is at the bottom of all the symptoms the self-help books try to fix. The Bible teaches that we have a problem that's bigger than the symptoms of dysfunction.

In this passage, Paul is answering the question about why the Gentiles should be held accountable for disobeying God when they weren't given His law. Here is Paul's indictment on all humanity:

21 *For though they knew God, they did not glorify Him as God or show gratitude. Instead, their thinking became nonsense, and their senseless minds were darkened.* 22 *Claiming to be wise, they became fools* 23 *and exchanged the glory of the immortal God for images resembling mortal man, birds, four-footed animals, and reptiles.*

24 *Therefore God delivered them over in the cravings of their hearts to sexual impurity, so that their bodies were degraded among themselves.* 25 *They exchanged the truth of God for a lie, and worshiped and served something created instead of the Creator, who is praised forever. Amen.*

26 *This is why God delivered them over to degrading passions. For even their females exchanged natural sexual relations for unnatural ones.* 27 *The males in the same way also left natural relations with females and were inflamed in their lust for one another. Males committed shameless acts with males and received in their own persons the appropriate penalty of their error.*

28 *And because they did not think it worthwhile to acknowledge God, God delivered them over to a worthless mind to do what is morally wrong.*

Let's work our way through this passage. Verses 21-23 show us the base error of humanity—idolatry. What is idolatry? It's when we take whatever was meant to roll our affections toward the Creator and we let those affections terminate on what was created instead. We don't want God; we just want His stuff. That's the inclination of us all: "Forget You, God. I just want what You made."

How does God respond? Look at verses 24-25. Here we see God judging us by allowing us to go our own way. He delivers us over to our own desires. All humanity continues running down the path of self-centered living.

What does that look like? Watch what comes next in verses 26-28. Our sin manifests itself in sexual dysfunction. The reason he uses sexual immorality as an example is not because he believes this sin is worse than all others but because it's a classic example of how we take the design of creation and make it into an idol. We worship created things instead of the Creator. It's an inversion of God's intention. Likewise, marriage between a man and woman is intended to be a picture of God's pursuit of us in Christ. Sexual immorality, on the other hand, is an example of how we rebel against that picture. The example Paul uses here is homosexuality, yet the truth applies to all kinds of sexual practices outside of God's plan.

So in this passage, we find what the Scriptures say is wrong with humanity—we are idolaters. All of us. We rebel in various ways (and there is a litany of sins listed at the end of Romans 1), but the common theme is that all of us have sinned.

So what are some ways that we explain away and excuse our sexual sinfulness? Several "street-level" arguments for sexual sin apply to premarital sex, adultery, and any sex outside of biblical marriage as Jesus described it. Let's go through them quickly.

• My sexual choices aren't hurting anyone else.

I call this the Golden Rule idea. If it's not hurting anyone else, what could be wrong with it? If a guy is sleeping with his girlfriend and the two of them are consenting adults, why should the church condemn that behavior? Likewise, if a woman wants to be in a monogamous sexual relationship with another woman, why does it matter as long as it's not harming anyone else?

The truth is, sexual sin does harm us. It's a sin against the body. We also must remember that the Golden Rule (love your neighbor) is second to the greatest commandment (love God with your whole self). Jesus said clearly in the Gospel of John that those who love Him obey His commands (see John 14:15). In other words, "If you love Me, obey Me." When you place the Golden Rule within the framework of biblical teaching, you see that sexual sin is a sin against our own bodies and is ultimately a sign of our rebellion against the God who made us.

• We're all sinners, so who are you to judge?

Whenever Christians affirm Jesus' vision for human sexuality, we are often greeted with the comeback line "So you're perfect, then?" The critics have a point here. The Bible shows us up as sexual sinners—all of us. But the real issue is repentance. The question is not "Do I sin?" but "Am I walking in repentance?" Christians ought never to feel superior to others. We're sinners too. The question is about repentance. Are we turning from sin and embracing Jesus?

• Jesus never talked about homosexuality.

This objection is only half true. When it comes to dealing with the topic explicitly, Jesus did not speak to the subject. But there is a sense in which Jesus did address this issue. In Matthew 15:18-19, we read: "But what comes out of the mouth comes from the heart, and this defiles a man. For from the heart come evil thoughts, murders, adulteries, sexual immoralities, thefts, false testimonies, blasphemies." The word for "sexual immoralities" covers all sorts of behaviors condemned in the Old and New Testaments.

Furthermore, when asked about divorce, Jesus went back to God's design in creation to show how men and women were to relate to one another. In the Sermon on the Mount, Jesus built on the Old Testament understanding of morality and even went beyond it—calling us out for lust.

• Sexual promiscuity is seen in nature.

Sometimes people will condemn faithfulness between a husband and wife (monogamy) or the Christian view of homosexual behavior by appealing to nature. As long as animals aren't monogamous and as long as we see some animals behaving in same-sex ways, then why would we condemn adultery or homosexuality or sex outside of marriage? If it's in nature, it must be natural.

This line of thinking denigrates the dignity of human beings, implying we are nothing more than our sexual passions. If we roll that argument out, we arrive in a scary place. We know of certain insects where the male impregnates the female and the female turns around and eats the male. Who wants that as the norm for humans? What's worse, those who believe in evolutionary theory adopt the principle "survival of the fittest." Do we want to imply, for example, that people with same-sex attractions are genetically weaker than other human beings? Of course not! Appealing to nature to justify any kind of sexual immorality is a dead end leading us to see people with less dignity, not more.

Respond to sexual sin with repentance and faith (Luke 5:29-32).

29 *Then Levi hosted a grand banquet for Him at his house. Now there was a large crowd of tax collectors and others who were guests with them.* 30 *But the Pharisees and their scribes were complaining to His disciples, "Why do you eat and drink with tax collectors and sinners?"*

31 *Jesus replied to them, "The healthy don't need a doctor, but the sick do.* 32 *I have not come to call the righteous, but sinners to repentance."*

So far we've seen God's original design for human sexuality. We've seen how we are all sexual sinners in need of God's grace. Now we will look at what our response ought to be. Christ calls us to respond to sexual sin (indeed, all sin!) with repentance and faith.

Sin didn't take Jesus by surprise. He was the friend of sinners. Before we can be a friend to sinners, we need to realize that Jesus is a friend to us. We are the sinners who need His salvation.

I tell everyone who struggles with temptation and sexual sin the same thing. We must humble ourselves before God every day, ask for His mercy, and hold tight to the promise that in Christ He has given us all the grace we need to be obedient to all His commands. It is not the nature and character of God to put us in situations where we cannot overcome temptation.

Throughout church history, many leaders have described our ongoing struggle against sin in two ways: *vivification* and *mortification*. Vivification is building yourself up in Christ and filling your life with whatever helps you see Christ as beautiful. Mortification is putting to death your sin, guarding your heart, avoiding places of temptation, and seeking out accountability with Christian friends. So on the one hand, you fill your life with whatever stirs your affections for Jesus. And on the other hand, you make war against your remaining sin.

Along the way, recognize that the church is meant to be an honest, open community for people fighting sin. We must be willing to confess our sin. When something is in the dark, it gains power. But when sin is brought out into the light, it loses some of its luster. The struggle continues, but walking in community aids our pursuit of holiness. We repent of our sin and trust God and the power of His Spirit.

How should we respond to non-Christians who have chosen to live outside of God's design and plan and act in ways that the Bible calls sinful? These situations come up all the time. We have friends committing adultery, coworkers living together but not married, gay and lesbian relatives.

Our response...love them anyway. Like Jesus, we should be a friend to sinners—He is to us. We must not justify or excuse sinful behavior nor avoid people living outside of God's plan. They are created in God's image and should be loved and treated accordingly—as people with inherent dignity (and we may need to defend that dignity when others act differently).

Our life goal is not to get people to stop sinning; it's to see people know and respond to the love of God, first and foremost. Changing behavior is what comes after Jesus has changed a heart. Our message is the gospel of Jesus Christ, not just traditional morality. Let's speak with our lips and model with our lives the love of Jesus Christ. We have a loving Father who desires our joy. We have a Savior who gave His life for our sins. We have the Holy Spirit who intercedes for us and empowers us to live in obedience.

Conclusion

We have looked at God's design for human sexuality as described in the Scriptures. We should always remember that sexuality is a gift from God. He wants our joy. When we disregard His commands, we are abandoning our own joy in order to pursue a lie. But when we respond with repentance and faith, we become a people full of compassion and grace. A people who love Jesus and hate their sin. A people who embrace the truths of God without compromise while loving those who disagree with us without condition.

Devotions

GOD'S DESIGN FOR SEXUALITY

In this chapter we look at God's design for sexuality. Christians often stay away from controversial subjects like this one. Maybe it's because anytime the news media addresses the Christian view of sex, they find people on the fringe of both sides of the issue and put them on television together. Rarely are Christians given the opportunity to share what God's design for sexuality is and why it matters.

As believers, we need to live with compassion toward those who disagree with us. Whenever we talk about sexual immorality (all kinds), we are not talking about issues only but people. We have family members, sons and daughters, brothers and sisters who have chosen to reject God's commands regarding sexuality. But even when we disagree on these "hot debates," we must address others as men and women created in the image of God.

At the end of the day, we are not called to win arguments. We're seeking to win people. We want to see the Holy Spirit convict people of sin and bring them to repentance. It's to that end we pray. At the same time, we want to live faithfully as Christians in a society that is sex-saturated. It is becoming more and more difficult to proclaim the biblical view of sexuality because our culture is quickly determining that our views are repressive, backward, and intolerant.

What should our response be? Love without compromise. We submit to the gracious commands of God and call others to repentance and faith.

Pause and Reflect

1   Are you willing to pay a social price for standing apart from the world when it comes to your views on sexuality?

- -

2   Are you open, honest, and seeking accountability about your own sexual sins?

Going After the Heart

Jeremiah 17:9: "The heart is more deceitful than anything else, and incurable—who can understand it?"

Sometimes the church feels like a trauma center. When we ask God to send us broken, hurting people to proclaim the gospel to, He usually does. It's messy. At times, it's exhausting. But watching God work in the severely wounded is a beautiful thing.

One of the most important things we can do when helping people recover from all kinds of brokenness is making clear the main problem. Whatever you think the problem is will determine how you try and solve it. Unfortunately, what happens in our society is that most people spend all their efforts on symptoms rather than the disease that's causing those symptoms.

The gospel goes after the heart. I am always amazed at how so many people have separated their actions from their hearts. Christians are guilty of this too. There is a reason you have a crummy marriage, lack patience, are always angry, and addicted to whatever. There is a reason you have to tear down others constantly and why you feel led to point out flaws and failures.

The reason is that our hearts are idolatrous and in need of God's redemption. If we simply try to handle the symptoms without addressing our heart as the source of those symptoms, we won't make progress in our ongoing growth in holiness. The good news of the gospel is that God has given us His Spirit, showering us with grace that changes our hearts, not just rules that manage our behavior.

Pause and Reflect

1 What are some of the sins you struggle with as a believer?

----

2 What are the ways that you apply the truth of the gospel to your ongoing struggle with sin?

You Can't Catch Sin

Sometimes, in our zeal to maintain our own purity and holiness, we conscientiously avoid spending time with people engaged in sexual immorality. But when we look at Luke 5:27-32, we see that Jesus spent time with people the religious elite had written off. He was welcoming and loving but not affirming of their sin. He called them to repentance.

Here's the truth—If you're going to be on mission, you're going to have to befriend lost people. Simple as that. You can't catch sin. You don't catch sin by hanging out with sinners. Don't forget, you're still a sinner too. Yes, you are saved by grace and you now have the presence of the Holy Spirit. You're no longer a slave to sin, but you cannot look down on others with an air of superiority. After all, salvation is a gift of God's grace.

If we're going to model the way of Jesus as we engage in mission, we must stand firm against sin even as we welcome and love sinners. So talk with people. Engage in dialogue. Almost all of my dialogue with people outside the faith is about the nature and character of God. Is it the desire of God to crush us? Is God glorified and exalted when we are merely trembling before Him and obeying out of fear or when we are filled with joy as we delight in living according to His commands? What is God like? What's He after?

Introduce people to Jesus. You can't catch sin. But He can. He takes people's sins all the time and puts them on Himself. And then He gives us His righteousness as a gift so we can stand before God unashamed, washed clean by the precious blood of the Lamb.

Pause and Reflect

1   What kinds of dialogue do you have with unbelievers?

- -

2   Do you intentionally seek to show hospitality to unbelievers?

- -

3   How can you maintain firm convictions on sexuality while also showing love to people who engage in different kinds of sexual immorality?

Discussion Questions

1   What are some of the flashpoints in our culture that lead to big debates about human sexuality? How is this subject treated when a biblical worldview is absent?

----

2   What are some problematic ways Christians have addressed sexual immorality in the past? Is it ever appropriate to address just one type of sin?

----

3   Why is it important that we understand God's commands in light of His character as a loving God who desires our joy?

----

4   In what ways can Christian couples model the beauty of Genesis 2:15-25 through their lives of love?

----

5   Why do the moral values accepted by society change and shift from generation to generation? In what ways does a scriptural view of morality as revealed challenge our culture's view of morality by consensus?

----

6   Do you think of sex as an idol in our culture? How does our sexual sinfulness reveal the idolatry in our own hearts?

----

7   What is the difference between attractions and behaviors? Why is it important for Christians to deny all sinful desires?

----

8   What arguments for immoral sexual behavior have you heard from people in your circles? How can we answer these arguments in ways that speak to the reality of our own sinfulness and need for God's grace?

----

9   Why is it important first to see ourselves as needing Jesus to be a friend to us before we see ourselves as friends to other sinners? What are some practical ways to implement vivification and mortification in our lives?

----

10 What is the role of the church in helping individual Christians walk in sexual purity? In what ways can the church be a place where sexual sinners find salvation in Christ and brothers and sisters in Christ find grace and support?

Chapter 11

By Jarvis Williams

Marriage

A God's-Eye View of Marriage

VOICES FROM *Church History*

"It is not your love that sustains the marriage, but from now on, the marriage that sustains your love." [1]
–Dietrich Bonhoeffer (1906-1945)

VOICES FROM *Church History*

"Our Lord always touches the most sacred human relationships, and He says—You must be right with Me first before those relationships can be right." [2]
–Oswald Chambers (1874-1817)

"Until death do us part"—serious words that far too many people fail to take seriously.

Marriage is one of God's greatest gifts to us. But in the current cultural climate, the lifelong commitment of marriage has been damaged. Divorce is prevalent in our culture (and sadly, in our churches). Our society is quickly redefining marriage as a contractual agreement that no longer takes gender into consideration: male and male, female and female. Marriage is one of our culture's "big debates."

In light of contemporary trends regarding marriage, Christians must return to the Bible to seek God's perspective on the marital covenant. It is not enough to view the Bible through our personal experiences of marriage. Instead, we must view our experiences through the lens of God's revealed Word.

In this chapter, we will consider a God's-eye view of marriage. Marriage is a lifelong commitment between one man and one woman. Marriage has practical ramifications for the way we live. Best of all, marriage provides a picture of the relationship between Christ and His church. In an age when many have lost sight of God's gift of marriage, we as Christians must faithfully seek to adhere to what God says is true about marriage and the family.

Marriage is a lifetime commitment between one man and one woman (Matt. 19:1-9).

Christians must submit to the authority of the Bible when seeking to discern God's view of marriage. The cultural climate of today—and any age, for that matter—changes along with the weather, but God's Word remains the same.

Today, two of the most debated aspects of marriage concern its dissolution (divorce) and its definition (union of a man and woman vs. same-sex marriage). But the Bible speaks to both, giving us clear statements about marriage that are both instructive and prescriptive for Christians today.

With respect to divorce, a debate raged even in Jesus day—what were the grounds for divorce? Were there a wide range of factors that could provide occasion for a husband to divorce his wife, even so far as a "no-fault divorce"? Or were the grounds very limited to only the occasion of sexual immorality? It was in this context that Pharisees approached Jesus with a question about divorce. But Jesus responded with teaching about marriage:

1 *When Jesus had finished this instruction, He departed from Galilee and went to the region of Judea across the Jordan.* 2 *Large crowds followed Him, and He healed them there.* 3 *Some Pharisees approached Him to test Him. They asked, "Is it lawful for a man to divorce his wife on any grounds?"*

4 "Haven't you read," He replied, "that He who created them in the beginning made them male and female," 5 and He also said:
"For this reason a man will leave
his father and mother
and be joined to his wife,
and the two will become one flesh?
6 So they are no longer two, but one flesh. Therefore, what God has joined together, man must not separate."
7 "Why then," they asked Him, "did Moses command us to give divorce papers and to send her away?"
8 He told them, "Moses permitted you to divorce your wives because of the hardness of your hearts. But it was not like that from the beginning. 9 And I tell you, whoever divorces his wife, except for sexual immorality, and marries another, commits adultery."

First, we should note that Jesus saw marriage as a lifelong commitment. In this passage, the Pharisees approached Jesus with a specific question about divorce: "Does the Law of Moses permit a man to divorce his wife for any reason?" Jesus responded to their question not by appealing to the opinions of the religious groups in His day but by going all the way back to the creation narrative in Genesis 1–2. His answer, quite simply, was no. A man cannot divorce his wife for just any reason.

The persistent Pharisees countered Jesus' answer with a text from Deuteronomy 24:1-4, in which the Law of Moses gave instructions for divorce. But Jesus went to the heart of the matter. He claimed that Moses permitted divorce because of the hardness of the people's hearts. Even so, Moses did not condone divorce because lifelong commitment was God's original plan for marriage (as seen in the creation story).

Jesus didn't lower the standard. He went back to God's vision for marriage when He said that no man was permitted to divorce his wife unless she was guilty of adultery. It is clear from Jesus' response to the Pharisees that Jesus saw marriage as a lifetime commitment between a man and a woman.

It is important to remember that Jesus' answer to the Pharisees was not just an isolated response. His comments here about divorce and remarriage occur in the context of His teaching on the kingdom of God. The surrounding context helps us understand that Jesus intended the citizens of the kingdom of God (Christians) to honor God's plan for marriage.

Second, we should note that Jesus explicitly affirmed the Bible's view of marriage as a lifelong covenant between a man and a woman. Therefore, as an institution created by God, governments (and the societies that they govern) may choose whether or not to recognize and affirm God's definition of marriage, but they cannot determine a definition of their own.

Marriage is practical (1 Cor. 7:1-9).

Marriage is not just an ideal. It has ramifications for the way we live. Marriage is practical, a truth that becomes evident in 1 Corinthians 7. The apostle Paul's remarks about marriage in this chapter were in response to the Corinthian Christians' questions about marriage. Paul took this opportunity to make a larger argument pertaining to Christians remaining faithful to Christ in the particular status in which God called them to faith (1 Cor. 7:17). Take a look at what Paul said about marriage:

1 *Now in response to the matters you wrote about: "It is good for a man not to have relations with a woman."* 2 *But because sexual immorality is so common, each man should have his own wife, and each woman should have her own husband.* 3 *A husband should fulfill his marital responsibility to his wife, and likewise a wife to her husband.* 4 *A wife does not have the right over her own body, but her husband does. In the same way, a husband does not have the right over his own body, but his wife does.* 5 *Do not deprive one another sexually—except when you agree for a time, to devote yourselves to prayer. Then come together again; otherwise, Satan may tempt you because of your lack of self-control.* 6 *I say the following as a concession, not as a command.* 7 *I wish that all people were just like me. But each has his own gift from God, one person in this way and another in that way.*

8 *I say to the unmarried and to widows: It is good for them if they remain as I am.* 9 *But if they do not have self-control, they should marry, for it is better to marry than to burn with desire.*

The first practical thing that Paul said in this passage about marriage is that Christians are free to remain single if they choose (v. 1). This is what he meant by affirming the view that "it is good for a man not to have relations with a woman." However, Paul quickly clarified that it is wise for men and women to marry because of the temptation of sexual immorality (v. 2).

Next, Paul urged husbands and wives to engage in regular sexual relations with one another within the context of their marital covenant. Far from seeing sex as a dirty or bad thing, Paul saw it as an important aspect of expressing faithfulness to one another in marriage. That's why he warned husbands and wives against depriving each other of sexual pleasure. Even when a couple may temporarily agree to abstain from sexual relations with each other in order to devote themselves to fasting and prayer, they should limit the time frame and plan to come together again in sexual union.

To state it bluntly, one reason God gave the gift of marriage was so that husbands and wives could enjoy sexual pleasure with each other. Paul's theology of sex and marriage is very simple—sex is only to be enjoyed within the covenant of marriage, and married people should engage in sexual relations with one another regularly.

Marriage also has ramifications for the way we treat one another—sexually, spiritually, and physically. One of the most practical components of marriage is the way it provides Christians with a God-honoring, Christ-exalting way to exercise and release their sexual passions.

At the same time Paul affirmed marriage, he also made it clear that singleness is a God-honoring status to which and in which God calls some to faith in Jesus Christ (1 Cor. 7:7,17). Paul claimed it is good for people to remain single and to focus their attention solely on living for Christ, just as he himself remained single and devoted his life to ministry.

Singleness brings its own blessings and challenges. A call to be single does not guarantee that sexual desire will be taken away. To put it in Paul's words, single people may burn with sexual passions and therefore should consider marriage (7:9).

God gives the gift of singleness to some. With this gift, He likewise gives the needed grace to overcome sexual temptation. But sexual passions and inclinations are still present within the hearts of single people, and those called to be single will still be tempted with sexual sin as long as they live in a fallen world. The church is called to come alongside those who are single and to encourage and exhort them in their desire to remain faithful to God's commands.

Marriage provides a picture of Christ and the church (Eph. 5:22-33).

Marriage provides a picture of the relationship between Jesus Christ and His bride, the church. Paul made this truth abundantly clear in Ephesians 5:22-33. Unfortunately, the way he spelled this out is hotly contested today. Many in our society put forth a view of marriage in which husbands and wives are interchangeable, but the Scriptures clearly affirm that marriage was intended to paint a picture of Christ and the church through the way husbands and wives interact with each other.

When we read Paul's remarks about marriage, we must not forget that they are part of his larger argument that the Ephesians (Gentile converts from paganism) must no longer conduct themselves as they once did. They were to put off their old selves (4:22). Instead, they must put on the new self that conforms to the likeness of God—Jesus Christ (4:24). Paul wanted the Ephesians to be godly. One way to live in a godly manner and imitate God and Christ (5:1-2) is to honor God's plan for marriage set forth in Ephesians 5:22-33 because marriage reflects the relationship between Christ and His church.

22 *Wives, submit to your own husbands as to the Lord,* 23 *for the husband is the head of the wife as Christ is the head of the church. He is the Savior of the body.* 24 *Now as the church submits to Christ, so wives are to submit to their husbands in everything.* 25 *Husbands, love your wives, just as Christ loved the church and gave Himself for her* 26 *to make her holy, cleansing her with the washing of water by the word.* 27 *He did this to present the church to Himself in splendor, without spot or wrinkle or anything like that, but holy and blameless.* 28 *In the same way, husbands are to love their wives as their own bodies. He who loves his wife loves himself.* 29 *For no one ever hates his own flesh but provides and cares for it, just as Christ does for the church,* 30 *since we are members of His body.*
31 *For this reason a man will leave*
    his father and mother
    and be joined to his wife,
    and the two will become one flesh.
32 *This mystery is profound, but I am talking about Christ and the church.*
33 *To sum up, each one of you is to love his wife as himself, and the wife is to respect her husband.*

Paul's exhortations to husbands and wives in Ephesians 5:22-33 are part of the "household code" of Ephesians 5:22–6:9. Paul addressed husbands and wives (5:22-33), children and parents (6:1-4), and slaves and masters (6:5-9) because these groups constituted a typical household structure in the Greco-Roman world, including even Christian households.

The household was a very important social structure in Paul's time. If the household were out of order, entire societies could be in chaos due to lack of harmony since the household was to reflect the larger society.

Wives

First, Paul called on wives to submit to their husbands (5:22). The term "submit" here basically means to recognize the authority of another. Sometimes interpreters of this verse fail to realize that Paul earlier commanded all Christians to submit to one another out of reverence for Christ (5:21). So what does mutual submission look like in the context of a home? Here we get a picture of God's intention for the family.

According to Paul, the husband is the head of the wife just as Christ the head over the church (5:23). Major debate persists today over the meaning of the term "head" in this passage. Some believe "head" means authority. Others believe it means "source." Regardless of one's interpretation, it is clear that Paul intended to parallel the headship of a husband with Christ's headship over the church: "And He put everything under His feet and appointed [Jesus] as head over everything for the church, which is His body, the fullness of the One who fills all things in every way" (1:22).

Interpreters must keep in mind that Paul was using an analogy, and all analogies break down when pressed too far. Even within this passage, Christ is said to be the Savior of the body, the church (5:23), but in no way can a husband be called the savior of his wife. But Paul's basic point is clear—a wife should submit to her husband.

What such submission looks like is not clearly developed in the text. Consequently, interpreters (especially men!) need to approach the application of this text with the utmost care and with both the glory of God and the good of their wives as the goal of all application. Without this concern they can misuse this text to advance their own agenda or as an excuse to belittle their wives.

Husbands

Ephesians 5:25-30 emphasizes that marriage between one man and one woman is not all about the husband and his needs. Here Paul commanded husbands two things: to love their wives as Christ loves the church and to love them as they love their own bodies. These commands were radical in the first century, for the prevalent view was that the woman should always in all circumstances submit and serve her husband without any expectation of mutual sacrifice placed upon the husband.

Husbands should especially feel the weight of Paul's first command! He wanted them to love their wives "as Christ loved the church." This doesn't simply mean that husbands should serve their wives (although it does mean that) but also that husbands should be willing to die for their wives, for this is how Christ displayed the ultimate expression of His love for the church. Husbands must live sacrificially and selflessly for their own wives.

In Ephesians 5:31, Paul grounded his exhortations in the creation narrative of Genesis 1–2 by asserting that a man (not a woman) shall leave his father and mother and be joined to his wife, and the two will become one flesh. In the ancient world, married couples often moved in with the parents, or vice versa. Thus, Paul was not simply speaking with reference to a geographical relocation of the husband away from his family. Instead, Paul believed the husband's fundamental obligation and priority in his life should no longer be his parents but his wife.

Paul supported this interpretation when he quoted from Genesis that the husband and wife become one flesh. The one-fleshness of the husband and the wife accentuates Paul's earlier remarks in Ephesians 5:28-30, that the husband must love his wife as he loves himself because they are one flesh. The husband's love for his wife must transcend all other loves and commitments in this world, apart from his love for and commitment to Jesus Christ. This is a great mystery, but when husbands love their wives in this way, they beautifully reflect the sacrificial and selfless love that Jesus Christ has for the church He died for.

Conclusion

As debates in society swirl over the nature and meaning of marriage, the Bible is clear. God sees marriage as a lifelong commitment between one man and one woman. He sees both marriage and singleness as different ways of expressing the beauty of the gospel. And He sees the interaction between husbands and wives as a picture of Christ's relationship to the church. If Christians want to have a God-centered, Christ-exalting view of marriage, we must look to the Bible to see God's design and direction.

Devotions

As Christ Loves

As a Christian husband, there is no greater demand placed upon me than Paul's remarks in Ephesians 5:25. If Paul would have simply said, "Husbands, love your wives," then this verse would not be vexing to me as a Christian husband. But when he added the short phase "just as" and followed with the words "Christ loved the church and gave Himself for her," he penned words that put a healthy fear within me regarding my role as a husband.

Too many husbands (including me) have viewed their role as one of being served as opposed to serving. But Paul reminded all Christian husbands that we should be willing to die for our wives if circumstances should require this. A vicarious death is the highest expression of Christ's love for His church and a husband's love for his wife, but Paul's remarks include more than death. They include a lifetime of selfless and sacrificial living on behalf of one's wife.

In Ephesians 5:28-29, Paul confirmed this interpretation by asserting that husbands should love their wives as their own bodies and that he who loves his wife loves himself, for no man (generally speaking) hates his own body. Husbands should always have the glory of God and the good of their wives in mind when they lead their families. Husbands must not rule their wives as evil tyrants who sit around and do nothing except complain and give demands. Instead, they should lead their wives by loving them in a selfless, God-honoring, and Christ-exalting manner by serving them, just as they love themselves.

Pause and Reflect
Husband, how often do you think of ways to serve your wife?

- -

1 Husband, how should the gospel impact the way you treat, serve, and love your wife?

- -

2 Husband, think of ways that you have failed to live out the command to love your wife as Christ loved His church, confess these sins to the Lord, ask for His forgiveness, and ask your wife for forgiveness.

As unto the Lord

Paul's admonition to women to submit to their husbands is increasingly offensive to people in our day. But "submit" in Ephesians 5:22 is not a negative, dirty word because Paul commanded the Ephesians to submit to one another out of reverence for Christ in the preceding verse. Thus, the exhortation to submit in Ephesians 5:22 continues the positive use of the word in Ephesians 5:21.

Paul also used the verb positively in Ephesians 1:22, when he asserted that God submitted all things under Jesus' feet. Thus, if Paul's command for wives to submit to their husbands in all things is a bad thing, then one must also argue that God's submission of all things under Christ's authority is a bad thing.

Regardless of the social, political, and cultural implications, Paul's remarks regarding submission are positive. A woman's respect and a husband's love both reveal the glorious relationship between Christ and the church, namely, submission and sacrifice. Consequently, Christian wives and Christian husbands should seek to discern how they ought to fulfill this command in the 21st century social context—simultaneously upholding God's design within marriage and pursuing everything that God has called them to be both within and outside of their marital context.

Both husbands and wives should go hard after God by means of prayer, Scripture reading, and other spiritual disciplines. With the power of the Holy Spirit, they can work together to pursue this command to submit and to love with a spirit of humility and selfless, sacrificial love first for Jesus Christ and second for their spouse.

Pause and Reflect

1 Take a minute and think of some practical ways that Ephesians 5:22 has been misused to abuse and oppress women.

----

2 Wife, how is God honored by you submitting to your husband?

----

3 Wife and husband, ask the Lord to expose ways in which you have both failed to obey Paul's commands in Ephesians 5:22-33, repent, ask Jesus for forgiveness, and ask each other's forgiveness.

WHY GET MARRIED?

To be married is a high calling. God demands and expects total loyalty between spouses. Such a high standard has caused many to reject the marital institution and instead to "shack up" with a companion.

Marriage is a commitment. When God calls a man and a woman to join together in matrimony, He is calling them to commit to one another until death. The commitment of marriage is explicitly stated in the creation narrative in Genesis 1–2, when God created Eve out of Adam and gave her to him to be his companion.

Let's be honest—Both God's expectations for marriage and Paul's remarks regarding marriage are difficult to fulfill. We all need God's supernatural help to honor God in our marriages and families. Marriage is not easy!

Shacking up with someone is an easy (though sinful) way to avoid commitment. But it fails to display God's glory to the world because it does not exemplify the relationship between Christ and His church. Shacking up with someone instead reflects the garden of Eden after sin entered the world, for this practice demonstrates that the creation is rebelling against God's original design by pursuing the opposite path created for the man and the woman in the context of marriage.

Pause and Reflect

1   Think of ways you and your spouse can more appropriately live out your marital covenant.

2   Husband and wife, read and pray through Ephesians 5:22-33 together.

3   If you're currently single and living immorally, repent, ask Christ for forgiveness. Then marry or move out!

DISCUSSION QUESTIONS

1   What are some of the most controversial aspects of the Bible's view of marriage in society today? Do these controversies affect your marriage? Why or why not?

2   How do our experiences impact our view of marriage? Why is it important to interpret our experiences through the lens of God's Word rather than God's Word through our experiences?

3   How can Christians lovingly minister to and support brothers and sisters who have been impacted by divorce? How does the gospel shape our response to divorce?

4   What are the contemporary views of marriage and divorce promoted in movies, music, media, and books today? In what ways does society's vision line up with Jesus' view of marriage? In what ways does it depart from Jesus' vision?

5   What are some practical implications of marriage for a husband and wife? In what ways does our relationship with God affect the way we treat our spouse?

6   What are the advantages and disadvantages of marriage when it comes to our role as citizens in God's kingdom?

7   In what ways can our churches minister to singles seeking to obey God's commands regarding sexuality? What are some of the practical benefits of remaining single?

8   In what ways does marriage reflect the relationship between Christ and the church? What do a wife's submission to her husband and a husband's sacrificial love for his wife look like in the 21st century?

9   How might Paul's remarks in 1 Corinthians 7:1-8 apply to widows or widowers? What are some ways the unmarried can show the beauty of the gospel?

10 How is our witness to the gospel of Jesus Christ damaged when Christian husbands fail to love their wives as Christ loves the church?

Chapter 12

By Adam Harwood

Human Life

The Sacredness of Human Life

VOICES FROM *the Church*

"Life is sacred and given to us by God; for that reason we must never condone the deliberate, unnatural taking of life."[1]
–Billy Graham

VOICES FROM *Church History*

"On the human level, Judas gave [Jesus] up to the priests, who gave him up to Pilate, who gave him up to the soldiers, who crucified him. But on the divine level, the Father gave him up, and he gave himself up, to die for us."[2]
–John Stott (1921-2011)

In *You Are Special*, Max Lucado tells the story of a land of wooden people, the Wemmicks. These people are all unique. Some have big noses; some have big eyes; some are just big, while others are short. Some wear hats and others wear coats.

The wooden people spend all their time assessing the worth of each other and placing stickers on each other. Beautiful, talented, and smart Wemmicks receive golden stars. Plain-looking Wemmicks with average ability and intellect receive gray dots. One day, a young Wemmick learns the secret of refusing to receive either the acclaim or disdain of his peers when he is introduced to the woodcarver, Eli.

Society rewards with attention people who have brains, bucks, or beauty. These are often the people popular at school or at work. Their faces grace magazine covers, their lives provide fodder for blogs and TV shows. They boast of millions of followers on social media platforms.

But do those traits (intelligence, wealth, and beauty) give a person more value than others? If so, then most people are not as valuable as the rich and famous. But what if the value of a person is found elsewhere? What is it that gives us value? And what are the implications for life and ministry?

In this chapter, we will learn that every human life, regardless of age or ability, has inherent value as an image-bearing creation of God. Taking the innocent lives of young, old, or weak humans through abortion or euthanasia is a sin against God and His image bearers. The good news is that the gospel provides the basis of human worth before God as well as the promise of forgiveness and healing for any person who repents and believes, including one who has taken an innocent human life.

Every human life has inherent value as an image-bearing creation of God (Jer. 1:5).

Jeremiah was probably in his early twenties when God called him to be a prophet. During a ministry spanning 40 years, Jeremiah addressed the nation of Judah (Jer. 2–45) and the nations surrounding Judah (Jer. 46–51). In 626 B.C., the 13th year of King Josiah's reign (Jer. 1:2), the word of the Lord came to Jeremiah:

> 5 *I chose you before I formed you in the womb;*
> *I set you apart before you were born.*
> *I appointed you a prophet to the nations.*

Before Jeremiah was even born, God chose, set apart, and appointed him to be a prophet. Notice that God said He formed Jeremiah in the womb.

Other biblical texts make similar claims. In Isaiah 44:2, the Lord is referred to as "your Maker who formed you from the womb." David declared that the Lord "knit me together in my mother's womb" and "my days were written in Your book and planned before a single one of them began" (Ps. 139:13,16). Luke 1:15 is a prophecy about John the Baptist, "He will be filled with the Holy Spirit while still in his mother's womb." Paul testified about himself in Galatians 1:15 that God "from my birth set me apart."

David, Jeremiah, John the Baptist, and Paul were assigned unique roles by God. God doesn't call every Christian to fulfill a ministry of kingly, prophetic, or apostolic calling, but we can still draw from these texts a principle that applies today as it did in their day.

God formed them in their mother's womb and had plans for them prior to their birth. The same is true of every person today. Every infant in the womb has inherent value as a special creation of God and should be regarded as a person with a future.

Additionally, every person is made in God's image. Genesis 1:26-27 declares, "Then God said, 'Let Us make man in Our image, according to Our likeness. They will rule the fish of the sea, the birds of the sky, the livestock, all the earth, and the creatures that crawl on the earth.' So God created man in His own image; He created him in the image of God; He created them male and female."

Some in our society believe that humans and animals have equal value and worth. One animal rights activist has denied that humans have special rights, saying instead, "A rat is a pig is a dog is a boy. They're all mammals."[3]

But the Bible makes a clear distinction between human life and the other kinds of life on earth. Humans of every age and ability have inherent value because each one is a special creation of God. Humans are unique among God's creation because only humans were endowed with God's image.

There are some who believe humans have value but say that a baby in the womb is not fully human. Others would question whether or not an elderly woman who depends on medication and assistance in a nursing home has as much value or worth as someone young and fit. For this reason, the youngest and oldest in society are in danger because they are not considered fully human.

But does this stand up to scrutiny? Not biblically. Not logically either. The SLED acronym, first developed by Stephen Schwartz, argues that a person's humanity does not depend on his or her size, level of development, environment, or degree of dependency.[4] (For more on the SLED acronym, see *The Case for Life: Equipping Christians to Engage the Culture* by Scott Klusendorf.)

S—Size

Infants in the womb are usually smaller than infants outside the womb. So? Children are usually smaller than teenagers. Women are usually smaller than men. Accountants are usually smaller than bodybuilders. But none of those groups are any more or less human because of their size.

L—Level of Development

Infants in the womb are less developed than toddlers both physically and mentally. Children are less developed than adults. Senior adults usually decline in their physical and mental abilities. None of those groups are any more or less human because of their level of development.

E—Environment

Are people fully human when they are under water? In an airplane? In a cave? Why would an 8-inch journey through a birth canal change the human nature of a person? If infants are human outside their mothers, then why should anyone regard them as non-human inside their mothers? People are people, regardless of their environment.

D—Degree of Dependency

Infants in the womb are dependent on their mothers. Similarly, newborns depend on their parents; mentally and physically disabled people depend on caregivers; and diabetics depend on insulin. Humanity is comprised of some people who depend on medicine or caregivers for their survival. This dependence makes them no less human.

Taking innocent lives of young, old, or weak humans through abortion or euthanasia is a sin against God (Gen. 9:5-6).

The Scriptures clearly teach that humans are made in God's image and therefore have innate value. It is no wonder, then, that the Scriptures condemn the shedding of innocent blood. This is why, following the account of the flood, God told Noah:

5 I will require the life of every animal and every man for your life and your blood. I will require the life of each man's brother for a man's life.
6 Whoever sheds man's blood,
his blood will be shed by man,
for God made man in His image.

The strict response God set down regarding the shedding of innocent blood is a clear picture of how seriously He takes murder. To sin against another human being in this way is a strike at the heart of God, for humans are made in His image.

The Bible speaks to the shedding of innocent blood in other places as well. In Jeremiah 32:35, for example, God declared it unthinkable that parents would sacrifice their children in an act of worship to the false god Molech. Jeremiah's statement (see also 7:31; 19:5) was not made because the child sacrifices surprised God; He has perfect knowledge of all future events. Rather, God was outraged and rebuked the action of the parents. He explicitly prohibited this ancient practice of child sacrifice (see Lev. 18:21; Deut. 12:31; 18:9-10).

Whenever we adopt the idea that some human beings are more valuable or more human than another, we are on a dangerous path. Eventually, some will recommend that the "less fit" members of society be eliminated in order to improve the human race. This view judges an individual's humanity based on "usefulness to society" or "quality of life"; a person who will be a drain on society's resources should be eliminated.

It sounds unmerciful and rather far-fetched, doesn't it? It's certainly unmerciful, but it is not far-fetched. The eugenics movement a century ago openly sought to eliminate the "unfit" through means of birth control and later through the targeting of African-American mothers for sterilization and abortion. World War II saw the horror of a civilized society (Germany) systematically killing those deemed "inferior," such as Jews, Gypsies, and homosexuals.

Even today, some studies show that 90 percent of infants diagnosed with Down syndrome through pre-term testing are aborted. [5] Bringing down the number of babies born with genetic issues due to correcting the genetic issue would be cause for celebration. But bringing down the number of births by ending those lives in the womb is an example of taking innocent lives.

Shockingly, infanticide (killing born-alive infants) is commonly discussed among scientists and philosophers as a good option for society. Princeton University medical ethicist Peter Singer argues, "When the death of a disabled infant will lead to the birth of another infant with better prospects of a happy life, the total amount of happiness will be greater if the disabled infant is killed. The loss of happy life for the first infant is outweighed by the gain of a happier life for the second. Therefore, if killing the hemophiliac infant has no adverse effect on others, it would, according to the total view, be right to kill him." [6]

Where does such a view come from? The denial of humanity's innate worth and value. Singer writes in *Pediatrics*, "We can no longer base our ethics on the idea that human beings are a special form of creation, made in the image of God, singled out from all other animals, and alone possessing an immortal soul." [7]

Worldviews matter. Ideas have consequences. If humans are no longer regarded as special creations of God who are made in His image, then they are wrongly considered disposable and replaceable. Tragically, this rejection of the inherent value of human life extends to the elderly and the weak. Although society considers growing old to be a curse, the Bible speaks of old age as a blessing from God (Ex. 20:12; Deut. 5:33; Prov. 16:31). Aging provides an opportunity to experience God's power in our weakness (2 Cor. 12:7-10).

In an article titled "Thank God for Aging," professor Chuck Dolph shows how God uses aging to sanctify us: "Aging strips us. If we live long enough, we will lose our beauty, our strength, our wealth, our independence, the control of our bodily functions, our pride, and perhaps our very self. These are our idols, all the things that we trust in life to make us attractive, valuable, and self-sufficient. If our aging is successful, we will end our lives stripped of everything but God, totally naked and helpless, utterly dependent on Him and the love of others. Everything that we trusted in life for our worth will have been stripped away. What a blessing to finally find our right relationship to God! Thank God for aging." [8]

The elderly and the weak have opportunities to experience God's power being perfected in their weakness. Because all human beings are valuable in God's eyes, we reject the taking of innocent lives—whether young or old, strong or weak.

Christ can forgive and heal anyone, including those who have taken an innocent human life (Acts 22:1-5; Rom. 8:1).

One of the greatest figures in Christian history was the apostle Paul. He was God's chosen instrument to deliver the gospel to the Gentiles (Acts 9:15). He planted churches throughout the known world. He wrote 13 of the New Testament books.

But listen to Paul's description of his life before coming to Christ:

1 *"Brothers and fathers, listen now to my defense before you."* 2 *When they heard that he was addressing them in the Hebrew language, they became even quieter.* 3 *He continued, "I am a Jewish man, born in Tarsus of Cilicia but brought up in this city at the feet of Gamaliel and educated according to the strict view of our patriarchal law. Being zealous for God, just as all of you are today,* 4 *I persecuted this Way to the death, binding and putting both men and women in jail,* 5 *as both the high priest and the whole council of elders can testify about me. After I received letters from them to the brothers, I traveled to Damascus to bring those who were prisoners there to be punished in Jerusalem.*

Before Paul served Christ and His church, he persecuted Christ and His church. Paul's pre-Christian life, when he was still known as Saul included persecuting believers to the point of death. Before his Damascus Road conversion (Acts 9:3-8; 22:6-21; 26:12-18), Saul attempted to serve God by arranging the arrest and persecution of Christian believers. He gave his approval of Stephen's martyrdom and then dragged other believers out of their homes and into prison (8:1-3). Saul had blood on his hands, as did other giants in biblical-redemptive history. Consider the lives of Moses and David.

But God's grace extends to people with blood on their hands. That is good news for all of us because the Bible teaches that Christ died for our sins. We are included among those who are responsible for the death of Christ. As Paul explained in Romans 5:8, "But God proves His own love for us in that while we were still sinners, Christ died for us!" Christ laid down His life by His own authority, according to the will of the Father. Still, Christ died for our sins (1 Cor. 15:3).

Paul, who had persecuted believers, preached a gospel that declared everyone in Christ to be free from condemnation. How did he view his life after coming to Christ? He wrote in Romans 8:1:

1 *Therefore, no condemnation now exists for those in Christ Jesus,*

In *Cradle My Heart: Finding God's Love After Abortion,* Kim Ketola explains, "Abortion strips us of the dignity of our unique role in producing human life, and wherever dignity has departed, shame resides." "Many of us have become spiritually confused after abortion, thinking we are being punished by God. We are sure that he hates us for what we have done. In our ignorance and fear, we may picture an angry judge, full of punishments that can never be satisfied. But endless condemnation is not part of God's plan for resolving our spiritual crisis. Jesus came to save the world, not condemn and destroy us." She continues, "No matter what your situation or issue, there is new life in Christ."[9]

Like the bleeding, ritually impure woman who reached out to Jesus and was healed and restored (Mark 5), Christ still heals women who are burdened by impurity and shame. Christ heals men who have failed to take responsibility for their actions. By coming to the Savior in repentance and faith, we can find forgiveness.

Conclusion

Do you remember the Wemmicks from our opening illustration? The main character of the story is a wooden doll named Punchinello. He learns that the value of a Wemmick does not go up with the stars he receives or go down with the dots. Each doll in the story is valuable because it was personally crafted by the woodcarver, Eli.

What might change in our thoughts or actions if we began viewing people as the Bible describes them, as special creations of God and bearers of His image? How might we view senior adults differently? How might we view the unborn differently? How might we view the physically disabled differently? Would this perspective lead us to treat them in different ways—even speaking and acting to defend their right to life?

The gospel compels us to action on behalf of the weak and needy. Just as God sent His Son to rescue us, vulnerable and perishing in our sinfulness, we are sent out for the sake of the vulnerable and the weak. We are on the front lines of the adoption movement. We provide a voice for the voiceless, sharing and showing the grace of a God who loves us all.

Devotions

GOD BECAME FLESH...
IN A WOMB

Ever seen ultrasound images of a baby in the womb? In the past, ultrasound technology provided grainy, black and white images. Pictures weren't printed because only doctors and nurses could see the baby's image. Today, 3-D and 4-D ultrasound technology provides amazing photos and video of babies in the womb.

Jesus, the Word of God (John 1:1), spent time in a womb. If there had been ultrasound machines in the first century, one could have been used to provide images of baby Jesus in the womb. Incredible thought, isn't it?

The Word could have come to earth in any number of ways. But God's plan was for Jesus to become flesh in a womb, be nourished in a mother's body, and then pass through a birth canal. Matthew and Luke are clear that no human male was involved at conception. But the rest of the process and time in the womb would have been the same as for any other infant. The Word became flesh...in a womb.

Does it matter that Jesus was fully human? Yes. Our salvation depends on it. Sinful people are made right with God only through the sacrificial and substitutionary death of the God-Man, Jesus. It was in the body of Mary that the Word became flesh (John 1:14).

Only the death of a perfect human could save mankind. That's precisely what happened at the cross. God made the perfect, righteous, sinless Jesus to be sin for us so we might become the righteousness of God in Him (2 Cor. 5:21). The atonement depends on Jesus being fully divine and fully human. Jesus became flesh to redeem flesh (Heb. 2:14-18). God became flesh...in a womb.

Pause and Reflect

1   Consider that the same Jesus who died for sin on the cross was once a baby in a womb.

- -

2   How does the humanity of Jesus inform your view of human worth?

- -

3   How does your understanding of the incarnation (enfleshment) of Jesus impact your view of a human mother's womb?

Psalm 139

I've known her for nearly twenty years, and she is a regular source of encouragement. She is a kind and gentle woman. She models trusting God, serving others, and loving her family—all in the twilight years of her life.

Betty's early years were difficult. Born during the "dust bowl" in Oklahoma, her childhood was filled with work and chores rather than fun and games. She once confided that she cared for her siblings and worked the fields but didn't feel loved as a child. That's why reading Psalm 139 as a young teenager was life changing.

She explained, "I recall reading the very first verse, which says the Lord knows me. Me? I couldn't believe the Lord would know me! I didn't feel special in any way. And I didn't feel loved. Why would the Lord want to know me? The chapter explains that He knows intricate details of my life. And I can't get away from His Spirit. That wasn't intimidating. Instead, it was overwhelming. I couldn't imagine why the God of the universe would be interested in knowing about me. Verse 13 explains that God created me. He knit me together in my mother's womb. It was overwhelming that I am—as is every other person—a special creation of God Himself. Wonderfully made (v. 14). Knowing me inside out, He still declares that His works are wonderful!"

God used Psalm 139 to bring my mother-in-law to Himself. He can use any passage of Scripture to reveal a person's need for Christ. It's interesting that the Scripture He used didn't threaten her with hell (although He has used those verses in the lives of other people). And the text wasn't a call to follow Christ (although she does follow Him). Rather, God revealed a young girl's need for a Savior by declaring her value as a special creation of God.

Pause and Reflect

1   How is the description of a person's value as described in Psalm 139 different than the world's narrative?

---

2   What are the differences between God-honoring and self-honoring views of our value as a person?

---

3   Think of the person whose company you least enjoy. Now reread Psalm 139 as a statement about that person. How should you respond?

THE SINFUL WOMAN

Have you ever met someone who felt unworthy to step into a church? She might joke that the roof of the church would fall in if she walked in the door. But the truth is that she feels unwanted and unloved by God.

In Luke 7:36-50, we see such a person. The whole town knew she was a sinner. Perhaps she had been with many men. Details of her sinful life were known widely. She lived in humiliation and shame.

When she entered the presence of Jesus in a Pharisee's home, she wept. Then she served Him. On her knees, she washed His feet with her tears and wiped them with her hair. Then she poured perfume on His feet. The town's notorious sinner was on her knees, broken and weeping at the feet of Jesus.

The woman's actions convinced the Pharisee that Jesus was not a prophet. The Pharisee reasoned that if Jesus were a prophet, then He would not have allowed her to touch Him. The Pharisee regarded himself too good to touch the woman. Because he thought of himself as needing very little forgiveness, he had very little love for Jesus (v. 47). It's not that the Pharisee didn't have many sins. Rather, he didn't think he needed much forgiveness. He was self-deceived. Not the woman. She was reminded of her sins daily. The community treated her like a spiritual leper.

Jesus used the contrast to teach on forgiveness and love. The woman's actions demonstrated that her sins had been forgiven. Why? She had a great love for Jesus because she knew she had been forgiven of many sins (v. 47). Much forgiveness? Much love. Little forgiveness? Little love.

Pause and Reflect

1   Who is the person at your school, work, or in your neighborhood that is viewed as the "sinful" person?

- -

2   In what ways might people today look down on a personal demonstration of love for Jesus?

- -

3   With whom do you more closely identify in the story and why: the Pharisee or the sinful woman?

DISCUSSION QUESTIONS

1   In keeping with the story of the Wemmicks, what kind of people would receive dots and what kind would receive stars by the following groups and why: classmates, coworkers, neighbors, family? In what ways can you relate the story of receiving stars and dots to your life?

2   Who or what assigns value to each human life? Family? Government? Culture? According to what standard is personal value measured?

3   What makes humans categorically different than rats, pigs, and dogs? What do you think it means for humans to be made "in God's image"?

4   What are the common reasons people give for justifying euthanasia or abortion? What do these reasons say about one's priorities?

5   What arguments have you heard that claim an infant in the womb is not fully human? How does the SLED acronym answer those arguments?

6   God was outraged by child sacrifice and strongly prohibited parents from sacrificing their children. What are the similarities and differences between ancient child sacrifice and abortion?

7   How might the birth of a child with a disability or your own aging be an opportunity to experience God's power and grace? In what ways can we in our church demonstrate our love and care for the elderly among us?

8   In what ways can Christians speak up for the unborn or show love and grace to the elderly?

9   God's Word declares no condemnation for those in Christ (Rom. 8:1), but Satan is called "the accuser" (Rev. 12:10). Have you ever been burdened by forgiven sin? How might a believer turn a discussion of the sanctity of human life to the gospel?

10 Why is it important to make sure that as we condemn the sin of abortion or euthanasia, we also speak of the loving kindness of God? What are some wrong ways we go about speaking of these issues?

Chapter 13

By Marty Duren

Christian Care

Concern for Others and the World

VOICES FROM *Church History*

"Redemption covers all aspects of creation, and the end of time will not signal an end to the creation but the beginning of a new heaven and a new earth: God will make all things new (Rev. 21:5)."[1]
–Charles Colson (1931-2012)

VOICES FROM *the Church*

"There's a great deal of giving that can take place even when I retain ownership—as long as I remind myself that God is the true owner, and I'm only his asset manager."[2]
–Randy Alcorn

For years, stewardship of the environment has not been considered an important issue for Christians. Perhaps because "going green" didn't seem to have eternal consequences or because "environmentalism" was viewed as the domain of Greenpeace activists who chained themselves to trees. Whatever the reasons, taking care of creation hasn't been high on the list of evangelical priorities.

On a similar note, we've sometimes overlooked God's call for us to care for the poor. Rightly concerned about Christians who have gradually abandoned evangelism in favor of feeding the hungry, we've tended to pull the pendulum back too far the other way—to forget the responsibility we have to care for the needy.

Whether the issue is care for creation or care for the poor, we ought to listen to what God's Word says to us. We cannot allow these discussions to degenerate into quick labels of "left" and "right," "liberal" and "conservative." God has something to say about these subjects, and we should adopt a posture of humility and obedience.

In this chapter, we will look at what the Bible says about our responsibility toward all of God's creation. God's love extends to what He has created and whom He has created. Our care for the planet is patterned after God's covenant with the earth after the flood. Likewise, the gospel forms us into the kind of people who are generous with our possessions. In giving to the needy, we show the love of Christ who gave up everything for our salvation.

God calls us to take care of His creation (Gen. 9:8-17).

When God created the heavens and the earth, He created them essentially good. This is why each day of creation ended with the affirmation, "And God saw that it was good." It was good for animals, good for plants, and good for humanity. It was good for bugs and every creeping thing that crawls on the earth.

God's call for us to take care of creation comes in the first chapter of the Bible, when God commanded Adam and Eve to rule over the earth wisely, to reflect His glory through their cultivation of the garden of Eden. Of course, in the biblical story line, we quickly see how God's creation was affected by human sin. Adam and Eve were forced to leave the garden. The earth is now not as it should be.

Still, creation is good. The prophet Isaiah clearly taught that God created the earth to be inhabited (Isa. 45:18). Paul described the entire creation as awaiting its redemption (Rom. 8:19-22). And Peter reminded persecuted believers that a new heaven and new earth will come (2 Pet. 3:13).

Just as God is redeeming those created in His image, He is redeeming the creation in which He placed us. Numerous prominent theologians throughout church history—from Irenaeus and Augustine through Luther, Calvin, and Wesley—have believed that our hope is for the redemption of all creation.

God's concern for the earth is made clear in His interaction with Noah after the flood in Genesis 9:8-17:

8 *Then God said to Noah and his sons with him,* 9 *"Understand that I am confirming My covenant with you and your descendants after you,* 10 *and with every living creature that is with you—birds, livestock, and all wildlife of the earth that are with you—all the animals of the earth that came out of the ark.* 11 *I confirm My covenant with you that never again will every creature be wiped out by the waters of a flood; there will never again be a flood to destroy the earth."* 12 *And God said, "This is the sign of the covenant I am making between Me and you and every living creature with you, a covenant for all future generations:* 13 *I have placed My bow in the clouds, and it will be a sign of the covenant between Me and the earth.* 14 *Whenever I form clouds over the earth and the bow appears in the clouds,* 15 *I will remember My covenant between Me and you and all the living creatures: water will never again become a flood to destroy every creature.* 16 *The bow will be in the clouds, and I will look at it and remember the everlasting covenant between God and all the living creatures on earth."* 17 *God said to Noah, "This is the sign of the covenant that I have confirmed between Me and every creature on earth."*

Whenever we recall the story of Noah and the ark, our conversations often focus on the cause of the flood (the sin of humanity), Noah's family (through whom God sustained humanity), and the number of animals on the ark. Barrels of ink have been poured out to estimate the dimensions of the ark and the source of that 40-day flood. (And why Noah did not kill those mosquitoes when he had the chance!)

VOICES FROM *the Church*

"Poverty alleviation is the ministry of reconciliation: moving people closer to glorifying God by living in right relationship with God, with self, with others, and with the rest of creation."[3]
–Steve Corbett and Brian Fikkert

A **GOD-CENTERED** WORLDVIEW

Far too infrequently, though, do we fully consider the covenant God made following the flood. God promised never again to destroy humanity, animals, or the earth with a flood. The rainbow serves as a sign of the covenant God made with humans (v. 9), animals (v. 10), and even the earth itself (v. 11).

God's covenant with Noah should inform the way we view the earth and the creatures of the animal kingdom. Our attitude toward God's creation should be the same as God's attitude. The psalmist revealed God's attitude in Psalm 145:9, "The LORD is good to everyone; His compassion rests on all He has made."

Deuteronomy 10:14 says the heavens, the earth, and everything in them belong to God, their Maker. Psalm 104 and Matthew 6:26-29 speak to God's provision and care for His creation. God made humanity to subdue and rule over His creation (Gen. 1:28) and placed them in the garden of Eden to cultivate it and watch over it (Gen. 2:15). Should we not follow the pattern and command of God to care for His creation?

God has a special purpose for the earth; it has a place in His eternal plan. Pursuing the heart of God should affect our attitude toward people, animals, and the earth itself. While we need not succumb to environmental extremism or the idea that nature is divine, our awareness of God's love for all He has made should create in us an attitude of honor and respect for God's creation. Romans 11:36 shows us how Christ's glory is involved: "For from Him and through Him and to Him are all things. To Him be the glory forever. Amen." "All things" certainly includes our terrestrial home, everything in it, and His image bearers who live here.

The sacrifice and resurrection of Christ was for the redemption of humanity and the renewal of the cosmos. Paul described the entire creation as waiting for restoration (Rom. 8:19-22). Far from neglecting or destroying His creation, God is reconciling it.

God calls us to manage possessions according to kingdom priorities (Matt. 6:19-21,24).

God has not only made us stewards of creation, He has also entrusted us with possessions we are to manage according to His priorities. Look at what Jesus taught about collecting treasures on earth:

19 *"Don't collect for yourselves treasures on earth, where moth and rust destroy and where thieves break in and steal.* 20 *But collect for yourselves treasures in heaven, where neither moth nor rust destroys, and where thieves don't break in and steal.* 21 *For where your treasure is, there your heart will be also.*

24 *"No one can be a slave of two masters, since either he will hate one and love the other, or be devoted to one and despise the other. You cannot be slaves of God and of money.*

Are you the type of person who has to have the latest and greatest of everything? Do you have to have the latest phone or tablet? Do your kids get every new video game system or brand-name jeans? Did you spend thousands of extra dollars on your last car just to have a certain package that was not really necessary?

We sometimes call the pursuit of such stuff "keeping up with the Joneses." The Bible calls it greed. Jesus called it covetousness. Covetousness is the sinful core of the heart that is devoted to things.

During His ministry, Jesus used plenty of illustrations to teach about His kingdom. He regularly used parables (the lost sheep, the lost coin) to spread the good news. He spoke of farmers, landowners, widows, property, barns, and harvest.

But when Jesus desired to draw a clear distinction regarding idolatry, He contrasted God and money. The language of slave and master is unmistakable. It is impossible both to serve God and the things God has put in our management.

It is worth noting the emotions involved when Jesus made this contrast. Hate, love, devote, and despise are not weak verbs! They are laden with passion. If a man tells his wife, "I love you!" it means something entirely different than "I hate you," but both are passionate and intense. Jesus did not leave open to us the possibility of dual allegiances.

We cannot serve two masters. The idolatry of money means that we love it and are devoted to it. Rather than it serving us for kingdom purposes, we serve it for temporal reasons. We use money to increase our earthly holdings, for laying up treasure where moth and rust can destroy it, when God has instructed us to lay up treasure in heaven.

Voices from *Church History*

"Money never stays with me. It would burn me if it did. I threw it out of my hands as soon as possible, lest it should find its way into my heart."[4]
–John Wesley (1703-1791)

Money and possessions should not be ends in themselves but means to an end. They directly compete for our attention and affection, distracting us from God's kingdom purposes. Money and possessions easily become idols because we can touch, taste, smell, see, and hear them. Contrary to the working of God, which is often intangible, possessions are tangible, and for that reason, we often find them easy to trust. That trust is idolatry.

A phrase we can use to describe our assignment on earth related to the possessions God has entrusted to us is *missionary manager*. We are missionary managers of all God has given us.

Jesus told His disciples, "As the Father has sent Me, I also send you" (John 20:21). God is a sending God, and we are a sent people. This *sentness* is directly related to how we handle the money and possessions God has placed in our authority. Viewing ourselves as missionaries (for which every decision concerning expenses, purchases, and possessions are subject to the mission) will change our saving and spending patterns.

A quick look through your online banking account page will reveal your heart. If restaurant expenses, clothing costs, car payments, hobbies, finance charges, and the like far outweigh offerings to your church, support for a homeless shelter, gifts given to the poor, financial support to stop human-trafficking, or money given to support the spread of the gospel, your master is clearly displayed.

As the famed pastor-martyr Dietrich Bonhoeffer said, "Earthly goods are given to be used, not to be collected. Hoarding is idolatry." [5]

God calls us to use our possessions to care for others (2 Cor. 8:1-4).

We've seen how God calls us to care for creation and to manage wisely the resources God has given us. One of the most important ways we exercise stewardship over the money and possessions He has entrusted to us is through generosity and care for others. Take a look at how Paul admonished the church in Corinth:

1 *We want you to know, brothers, about the grace of God granted to the churches of Macedonia:* 2 *During a severe testing by affliction, their abundance of joy and their deep poverty overflowed into the wealth of their generosity.* 3 *I testify that, on their own, according to their ability and beyond their ability,* 4 *they begged us insistently for the privilege of sharing in the ministry to the saints,*

In 2 Corinthians, Paul taught the Corinthian believers about God's grace and how it empowers generosity. To do this, he entreated them to learn from the believers in Macedonia. Those believers were poor beyond poor. Scripture says they were in "affliction" and in "deep poverty." Yet even though they were financially broke, they were spiritually wealthy. They begged Paul to include them in the opportunity to help other believers who were suffering, probably because of a famine.

These poverty-stricken believers were so passionate for God's kingdom ministry to the saints that they did not consider their generosity a sacrifice. It wasn't a burden but a joy! They considered it a privilege.

Christ's followers are never more like Him than when we are joyfully generous to those in need. He is the One who gave up heavenly riches and became poor for our sakes. Now it is our privilege to give of our possessions for the sake of those in need.

Not only do others need the blessing, we need the obedience. Those in poverty need to experience the compassion of Jesus; we need to be conformed to His image.

Western Christians enjoy a standard of living unparalleled, almost beyond imagining, in the annals of human history. While Americans debate how tax cuts or increases will affect our economy, the dollar amount alone involved in those taxes—never mind the remaining income—dwarfs the $1.25 and less a day that just over 20 percent of the world uses trying to scrape out a living. [6]

The danger we face from an incorrect attitude toward money and possessions is that it diminishes our willingness to help meet the needs of others or increase their opportunities to hear the gospel.

Integral with the gospel orientation of following Christ is a deep care for humanity. We are, of course, commanded to take the gospel to all nations (Matt. 28:18-20; Mark 16:15; Luke 24:46-49). But it does not stop with a transfer of information. Spirit-motivated expressions of compassion are the visuals of the kingdom.

The early Christians understood that living out the implications of the gospel included loving those neglected, shunned, or deemed unimportant by the world. The poor, the widow, the disparaged, and orphans were not simply a peripheral issue for Christians, not just poster fodder for guilt-induced offerings. They were the focus of Christian living and ministry.

Early Christians pooled many of their resources so that every believer had all they needed for living (Acts 4:34-35); offerings like the one mentioned above were received by believers in one area for believers in other areas (Rom. 15:26). After the apostles and elders affirmed Paul's apostleship, he remembered they "asked only that we remember the poor" (Gal. 2:10).

What opportunities do we have to show the love of Christ? In our town, a local homeless organization has created an opportunity for people who were recently homeless or may still be to become entrepreneurs. A bi-monthly newspaper provides an earning opportunity for these vendors who sell them on street corners—rain or shine, heat wave or cold front—all over the area. Even though the papers sell for only a dollar, from which the salesperson gets $0.75 (+ tips), it is amazing to see hundreds of people pass them by without any interaction at all, much less a purchase. My wife and I usually end up with multiple copies of each edition trying to support several vendors each month.

Exercising compassion toward those who do not know Christ is an expression of God's love. Through that expression they may come to know the God who so loved the world that He gave His only begotten Son to die for our sins.

Conclusion

Colossians 1:15-20 teaches us the centrality of Jesus the Messiah to the gospel. Everything was made by Him and for Him, everything is held together in Him, and He will ultimately reconcile everything.

The gospel is more than just information. It is good news. It is a story. It is the story of a God who loves the work of His hands and has provided everything needed to redeem and restore it. When we care for creation, manage possessions wisely, and demonstrate care and concern for others, we are mirroring the heart of God who loves us and loves His world.

Voices from *the Church*

"It is grace that justifies, grace that glorifies, and grace that sanctifies. The attitudinal journey from owner to manager is part of the sanctification process and is smothered in the undeserved goodness of God. The further step of giving as Jesus and Paul commend is also empowered by God's grace. Missional giving is not birthed from my own 'can do' attitude, but is a humble participation in God's mission."[7]

–Marty Duren

Devotions

LOVING CREATION

Our house sits on the perimeter of a 150-acre wood. The foliage is too thick to see through until fall arrives and the leaves are off the trees. Then we can see well into the ridges and hollows where deer, wild turkeys, opossums, finches, and bobcats live.

We've taken many trips to Alberta, Canada, to minister in a seminary there. The vista of the Canadian Rockies in the distance is a wonder to behold—mountains as far as the eye can see with summit after summit, climb after climb, and cliff after cliff. At times the view is worth more than a thousand words, but none sufficient can be called to mind.

The famed naturalist of the last century John Muir wrote of the Sierra Mountains: "The air is distinctly fragrant with balsam and resin and mint, every breath of it a gift we may well thank God for. Who could ever guess that so rough a wilderness should yet be so fine, so full of good things? One seems to be in a majestic domed pavilion in which a grand play is being acted with scenery and music and incense…God himself seems to be always doing his best here, working like a man in a glow of enthusiasm."[8]

Despite the tragic intrusion of sin, God's creation is still good. We dare not miss His wisdom, power, and strength in the middle of it. We dare not miss the witness or His promise. If we look at a forest and see only lumber, or at a field and envision only a subdivision, or at an animal and see only a beast of burden, we miss the sheer joy of the beauty, harmony, and uniqueness of that which reflects its Creator.

Pause and Reflect

1 What are some ways we might honor God for the creation He has promised to redeem and restore?

-----

2 How can we allow our appreciation for creation to become praise for the Creator?

-----

3 How can we avoid the temptation to idolize creation by giving it a level of priority God never commands?

SEEING PEOPLE AS GOD SEES

Have you ever caught yourself looking right through something only to be startled by something else in your surroundings? This happens to me often when sitting in traffic or looking out a window into the yard. Ultimately a car horn or my wife's voice brings me back to reality. Then I realize I was not really looking at anything. I was looking through it.

The Bible says numerous times in the Gospels that Jesus looked at the crowds or a person and had compassion. Jesus could not have had compassion on people if He had been looking through them; He was looking at them.

The most well-known story of compassion Jesus told is the story of the good Samaritan. In Luke 10 we are told a traveler was beaten and robbed while on the road from Jerusalem to Jericho. Two of his own people—Jewish folks—passed by without lending aid. These two were religious leaders!

Sometime after the assault, another traveler stopped to give him aid. The helper is identified as a Samaritan, a man of mixed heritage whom the Jews despised. He anointed and bound the hurt man's wounds, took him to a place to stay, and made arrangements to cover his expenses. From this Samaritan we learn the costs of compassion. Usually the investment involves time, energy, and often finances.

This is Christ's example of one person having compassion on another. Compassion is preceded by seeing people as God sees. We cannot live our lives looking through the people for whom Christ died. We must look at them with the eyes of Christ, determined to demonstrate His compassion whatever the time, energy, or financial cost.

Pause and Reflect

1   When is the last time you gave assistance to someone who had no hope of repaying you?

- -

2   When you help people who are struggling or who have given up, what kind of emotional response do you have? Brokenness? Joy? Bewilderment? Why?

Honoring God with Our Wealth

It has been said the only things we can take to heaven are the people we lead to Christ and the treasures we send ahead. The first part is rather easy to grasp, but the second might not be as readily understood. It is, however, affirmed by Jesus (see Matt. 6:19-21).

God is concerned about our wealth because wealth is an indicator of where our heart resides. If our hearts are with our wealth, they cannot be with God.

Jesus warned against collecting treasure on earth because of the ease with which it could be stolen or destroyed. Instead, He encouraged us to collect (or "lay up") eternal treasure that cannot be destroyed. One way we can do this is by honoring God with our wealth.

Honoring God with wealth means using money and possessions according to His priorities and, so far as we can discern, according to His kingdom purposes. We find this in obedience to what God teaches us about our attitude toward money: generosity instead of greed, sharing instead of hoarding, using it instead of being used by it, using it for mission instead of mammon. Any attempt to be gospel centered in other parts of our lives will be thrown askew if our finances are not subject to gospel centrality.

Sometimes overlooked in Jesus' words is the truth that our hearts follow our treasure. "Where your treasure is, there your heart will be," said the Savior. If we hoard it, our hearts are enslaved to it. If, however, we honor God by collecting treasure in heaven—even when our heart is not in it—sooner or later it will be.

Pause and Reflect

1   How is it a challenge to collect treasure in heaven rather than on earth?

2   Ponder how your heart follows your treasure. What are some of your conclusions?

3   Consider seriously any material possessions that have captured your heart. Take time to offer a prayer of repentance, asking God for His power to honor Him with all of your wealth.

DISCUSSION QUESTIONS

1   Do you think Christians give too much or too little thought to our responsibility to steward creation? What about our responsibility to the poor?

2   What are some ways environmentalism and reducing poverty get "politicized" in our society? How can we as Christians go beyond politics to address the issues from a biblical perspective?

3   How does God's plan of redemption affect the way we view things such as littering, recycling, endangered species, and the treatment of animals? How does God's care and compassion impact our view of these issues?

4   Why do you think some Christians are uncomfortable with the idea of creation care? Why must we be careful not to go along with those who would deify or worship the earth?

5   What are some signs that our hearts have been captured by our possessions? In what ways does the notion of "managing" rather than "owning" our possessions impact our view of them?

6   In what ways can we demonstrate a heart for God's mission? What does managing what God has entrusted to us look like when we are focused on His kingdom?

7   In your current giving practices, how do you respond when opportunities to give are presented to you? How do you decide when to give and when not to give?

8   Have you experienced generosity from someone less fortunate than yourself? How did that impact you? What is the difference between giving joyfully or begrudgingly? How does the gospel impact our motivation for giving?

9   Can you think of a time you sacrificed something valuable in order to help the poor? What about a time you neglected to help? Why is it important to demonstrate the power of the gospel through our care for others?

10 If you have children, what are some steps you can take to help ensure that they mature with a biblical view of money and possessions?

Endnotes

Chapter 1

1. C .S. Lewis, *The Weight of Glory* (New York: HarperCollins, 1949, rev. 1980), 140.
2. James Emery White, *A Mind for God* (Downers Grove: InterVarsity, 2009), 16.
3. Eric Geiger, Michael Kelley, and Philip Nation, *Transformational Discipleship* (Nashville: B&H, 2012), 93-94.
4. C. S. Lewis, *Mere Christianity* (New York: Touchstone, 1980), 119.

Chapter 2

1. G. Campbell Morgan, *The Gospel According to John* (New York: Revell, 1933), 270.
2. Ken Sande, *Resolving Everyday Conflict* (Grand Rapids: Baker, 2011), 49.
3. Ed Stetzer and Philip Nation, eds., "From Glory to Glory," in *The Mission of God Study Bible* (Nashville: B&H, 2012), 1217.

Chapter 3

1. Herschel H. Hobbs, *The Baptist Faith and Message* (Nashville: Convention Press, 1971), 23.
2. Adrian Rogers, *Adrianisms: The Wit and Wisdom of Adrian Rogers*, vol. 1 (Memphis: Love Worth Finding Ministries, 2006), 35.
3. Robert L. Plummer, *40 Questions About Interpreting the Bible* (Grand Rapids: Kregel, 2010), 57.
4. Josephus, *Against Apion*, in *The Life and Works of Flavius Josephus*, trans. William Whiston (New York: Holt, Rinehart and Winston, 1960), 861.
5. Robert L. Plummer, *40 Questions About Interpreting the Bible*, 61.
6. Matt Slick, "Manuscript evidence for superior New Testament reliability," CARM [online; cited 23 April 2013]. Available from the Internet: *carm.org.*

Chapter 4

1. Jonathan Pennington, *Reading the Gospels Wisely* (Grand Rapids: Baker, 2012), 71.
2. E. Y. Mullins, *Christianity at the Cross Roads* (New York: George H. Doran Company, 1924), 81.
3. Adapted from *40 Questions About Interpreting the Bible*, by Robert L. Plummer, 44-45.
4. Richard Bauckham, *Jesus and the Eyewitnesses* (Grand Rapids: Eerdmans, 2006), 5.

Chapter 5

1. Oswald Chambers, in *The Quotable Oswald Chambers*, comp. and ed. David McCasland (Grand Rapids: Discovery House, 2008), 140.
2. Erwin McManus, "Is Jesus the Only Way?" [online; cited 13 April 2013] Available from the Internet: *www.youtube.com/watch?v=CIfp07TMllM.*
3. D. A. Carson, *The Intolerance of Tolerance* (Grand Rapids: Eerdmans, 2012), 3.

Chapter 6

1. William Lane Craig, *Reasonable Faith* (Wheaton: Crossway, 2008), 71.
2. N. T. Wright, *The Resurrection of the Son of God* (Minneapolis: Fortress Press, 2003), 730.
3. Julian Baggini, "Yes, life without God can be bleak: Atheism is about facing up to that," *The Guardian* [online], 9 March 2012 [cited 14 March 2013]. Available from the Internet: *www.guardian.co.uk.*
4. William Lane Craig, *Reasonable Faith* (Wheaton: Crossway, 2008), 74.
5. C. S. Lewis, *Mere Christianity*, 45-46.
6. William Lane Craig, *Reasonable Faith*, 86.
7. Julian Baggini, "Yes, life without God can be bleak: Atheism is about facing up to that." Available from the Internet: *www.guardian.co.uk.*
8. Bertrand Russell, *Why I Am Not a Christian* (New York: Simon & Schuster, 1957), 107.

Chapter 7

1. Marva Dawn, *Talking the Walk* (Grand Rapids: Brazos Press, 2005), 125.
2. *The Book of Common Prayer and the Administration of the Sacraments and Other Rites and Ceremonies of the Church* (Episcopal Church) (England: Oxford University Press, 1897), 542.
3. Richard Dawkins, *The God Delusion* (New York: Houghton Mifflin, 2006), 51.
4. Barbara Hendrix, *Miracles in the Trash* (Bloomington, IN: Westbow Press, 2012), 153.
5. The Rhinoplasty Center, "Frequently Asked Questions About Rhinoplasty" [online; cited 6 May 2013]. Available from the Internet: *www.therhinoplastycenter.com.*

Chapter 8

1. Timothy Keller, *The Reason for God* (New York: Penguin, 2008), 30-31.
2. Charles Spurgeon, "The Rough Hewer," in *The Metropolitan Tabernacle Pulpit*, vol. 36 (London: Passmore & Alabaster, 1890), 151.

Chapter 9

1. Billy Graham, in *Billy Graham in Quotes*, ed. Franklin Graham (Nashville: Thomas Nelson, 2011), 175.
2. C. S. Lewis, *The Quotable Lewis*, eds. Wayne Martindale and Jerry Root (Carol Stream, IL: Tyndale, 1990), 293, 294.
3. Richard Dawkins, *The Blind Watchmaker* (New York: Norton, 1986), 116.
4. Charles Misner, quoted in *Think*, by John Piper (Wheaton: Crossway, 2010), 194.

Chapter 10

1. Francis Schaeffer, in *Letters of Francis A. Schaeffer*, ed. Lane Dennis (Wheaton: Crossway, 1986), 202.
2. Tim Chester, *You Can Change* (Wheaton: Crossway, 2010), 67.

Chapter 11
1. Dietrich Bonhoeffer, "A Wedding Sermon from a Prison Cell," in *Letters and Papers from Prison* (Simon & Schuster, 1997), Part 1.
2. Oswald Chambers, in *The Quotable Oswald Chambers*, comp. and ed. David McCasland, 160.

Chapter 12
1. Billy Graham, in *Billy Graham in Quotes*, ed. Franklin Graham, 215.
2. John R. W. Stott, *The Cross of Christ* (Downers Grove: InterVarsity, 2006), 64.
3. Ingrid Newkirk, quoted in *The Animal Rights Debate*, by Carl Cohen and Tom Regan (Lanham, MD: Rowman & Littlefield Publishers, 2001), 35.
4. Scott Klusendorf, *The Case for Life: Equipping Christians to Engage the Culture* (Wheaton: Crossway, 2009), 28-29.
5. C. Mansfield, S. Hopfer, and T. M. Marteau, "Termination rates after prenatal diagnosis of Down syndrome, spina bifida, anencephaly, and Turner and Klinefelter syndromes: a systematic literature review. European Concerted Action: DADA (Decision-making After the Diagnosis of a fetal Abnormality)." *Prenatal Diagnosis* (19 September 1999): 808-12; Abstract, by PubMed.gov [online; cited 3 June 2013]. Available from the Internet: *www.ncbi.nlm.nih.gov*.
6. Peter Singer, *Writings on an Ethical Life* (New York: HarperCollins, 2000), 189-90.
7. Peter Singer, "Sanctity of Life or Quality of Life?" *Pediatrics* 71.1 (July 1983): 129.
8. Chuck Dolph, "Thank God for Aging," *Cedarville Torch* 28.1 (Spring/Summer 2007): 12.
9. Kim Ketola, *Cradle My Heart: Finding God's Love After Abortion* (Grand Rapids: Kregel, 2012), 30-31, 74.

Chapter 13
1. Charles Colson, *How Now Shall We Live?* (Carol Stream, IL: Tyndale, 1999), 296.
2. Randy Alcorn, *Money, Possessions and Eternity* (Carol Stream, IL: Tyndale, 2003), 196.
3. Steve Corbett and Brian Fikkert, *When Helping Hurts* (Chicago: Moody, 2012), 78.
4. John Wesley, quoted in *Money, Possessions and Eternity*, by Randy Alcorn, 195.
5. Dietrich Bonhoeffer, quoted in *Money, Possessions and Eternity*, by Randy Alcorn, 327.
6. The World Bank, *World Development Indicators 2012* (Washington, DC: The World Bank, 2012), 2.
7. Marty Duren, *The Generous Soul* (Smyrna, DE: Missional Press, 2010), 94-95.
8. John Muir, *My First Summer in the Sierra* (New York: Houghton Mifflin, 1911), 80.

How to Use This Resource

Welcome to *The Gospel Project*, a gospel-centered curriculum that dives deep into the things of God, lifts up Jesus, focuses on the grand story of Scripture, and drives participants to be on mission. This short-term resource provides opportunities to study the Bible and to encounter the living Christ. *The Gospel Project* provides you with tools and resources to purposefully study God's Word and to grow in the faith and knowledge of God's Son. And what's more, you can do so in the company of others, encouraging and building up one another.

Here are some things to remember that will help you maximize the usefulness of this resource:

Gather a Group. We grow in the faith best in community with other believers, as we love, encourage, correct, and challenge one another. The life of a disciple of Christ was never meant to be lived alone, in isolation.

Pray. Pray regularly for your group members.

Prepare. This resource includes the Bible study content, three devotionals, and follow-up questions for each chapter. Work through the chapter and devotionals in preparation for each group session. Take notes and record your own questions. Also consider the follow-up questions so you are ready to participate in and add to the discussion, bringing up your own notes and questions where appropriate.

Resource Yourself. Make good use of the additional resources available on the Web at *www.gospelproject.com/additionalresources*. Download a podcast. Read a blog post. Be intentional about learning from others in the faith.

Group Time. Gather together with your group to discuss the chapter and devotional content. Work through the follow-up questions and your own questions. Discuss the material and the implications for the lives of believers and the mission to which we have been called.

Overflow. Remember…*The Gospel Project* is not just a curriculum. WE are the project. The gospel is working on us. Don't let your preparation time be simply about the content. Let the truths of God's Word soak in as you study. Let God work on your heart first, and then pray that He will change the hearts of the other people in your group.

Small Group Tips

Reading through this section and utilizing the suggested principles and practices will greatly enhance the group experience. First is to accept your limitations. You cannot transform a life. Your group must be devoted to the Bible, the Holy Spirit, and the power of Christian community. In doing so your group will have all the tools necessary to draw closer to God and to each other—and to experience heart transformation.

General Tips
• Prepare for each meeting by reviewing the material, praying for each group member, and asking the Holy Spirit to work through you as you point to Jesus each week.

• Make new attendees feel welcome.

• Think of ways to connect with group members away from group time. The amount of participation you have during your group meetings is directly related to the amount of time you connect with your group members away from the group meeting. Consider sending e-mails, texts, or social networking messages encouraging members in their personal devotion times prior to the session.

Materials Needed
• Bible

• Bible study book

• Pen/pencil

Provide Resources for Guests
An inexpensive way to make first-time guests feel welcome is to provide them a copy of your Bible study book. Estimate how many first-time guests you can expect during the course of your study, and secure that number of books. What about people who have not yet visited your group? You can encourage them to visit by providing a copy of the Bible study book.

Four Keys to Becoming a More Caring Group

How deeply do your group members care for and support each other? Developing a caring group is countercultural in the 21st century, but it must happen! Here are four keys to becoming a more caring group:

1. **Caring for each other is modeled by leaders.** Are you modeling a genuine caring attitude?
2. **Healthy transparency and vulnerability is modeled by leaders.** If you want your group members to be open about their needs, you'll often have to go first.
3. **Establish commitments, values, and expectations using a small group agreement.** Remember, genuine caring is countercultural and not on the radar of many group members.
4. **Make heroes out of group members who go out of their way to be caring.**

Adapted from "5 Keys to Becoming a More Caring Group," by Mark Howell, Bible Studies for Life blog [online], 12 April 2013 [cited 1 July 2013]. Available from the Internet: *blog.lifeway.com/biblestudiesforlife.*

The Missional Group

A small group that is missional is made up of individuals who are constantly on mission, praying for and discussing needs of people at work, in their neighborhoods, and anywhere else. And God inspires them with ideas to meet those needs. As a leader, you can guide your group to become missional by:

• Modeling missional living by seeing needs, meeting them personally, and then sharing with the group how it blessed you.

• Bringing missional opportunities to your group and allowing them to join you in ministry.

• Pointing out to your group members when gathered for Bible study that this is how the early church, and Jesus Himself, lived life.

• Inviting those transformed through contact with missional people or groups to share their testimonies in your group meetings.

Rick Howerton, "Is Your Small Group on Mission or Missional?" LifeWay.com [online], 17 December 2009 [cited 1 July 2013]. Available from the Internet: *www.lifeway.com.*

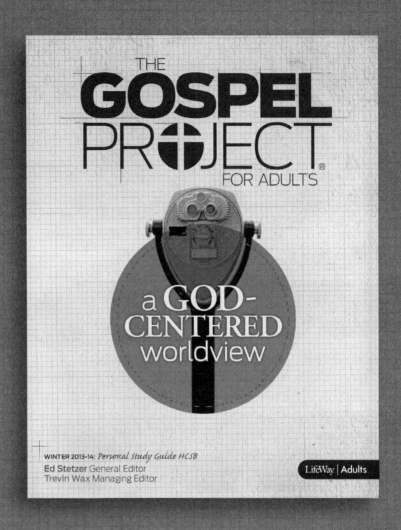

Continue the journey with The Gospel Project® ongoing studies...

Enjoying The Gospel Project? If your group meets regularly, consider adopting The Gospel Project as an ongoing Bible study series.